Using Business Maths

Using Business Maths

Robert Jordan

Gill & Macmillan

Gill & Macmillan
Hume Avenue
Park West
Dublin 12
with associated companies throughout the world
www.gillmacmillan.ie

978 07171 5715 0

Print origination by MPS Limited
Printed by GraphyCems, Spain

The paper used in this book comes from the wood pulp of managed forests. For every tree felled, at least one tree is planted, thereby renewing natural resources.

A CIP catalogue record is available for this book from the British Library.

To my dear wife, Maeve, who has quietly kept the show on the road, and to Rita Emmett, for her constant encouragement.

Acknowledgements

I would like to thank my editor, Kristin Jensen, for her patient and efficient work and quiet insistence on getting things right. Also Catherine Gough, Marion O'Brien and Jen Patton from Gill & Macmillan for their encouragement and handling of all the technical stuff. One must also mention the people behind the scenes, whose names I have never heard: designer, typesetter, printer and so on. Thanks to one and all.

I also want to thank my old school teachers from long ago, my colleagues Enda Connolly and Alan Dillon, who encouraged me to go ahead and write it, and my students over the past eight years, who have inspired me every day. I especially want to mention Sorin, who warned me that 'once I write it, I can no longer blame the textbook!'

Foreword

This book is designed to provide a complete text for two of the FETAC Level 4 modules: Business Calculations (4N2279) and Functional Mathematics (4N2138). Many of my adult students have benefited from the revision of some of their (largely forgotten) school maths provided by the old Level 5 Business Calculations Module. These modules and this text are designed to equip students with a practical, business-oriented set of maths skills while completing either of the FETAC modules.

Much of the material in this book is common to both modules, so I've arranged the chapters in the order that hopefully will make a seamless path through your course. Some teachers will therefore find some chapters, or parts of chapters, superfluous, depending on the module you're doing. The good news is that in my experience, students never complain when the teacher announces they are about to skip a section. I see this as a win-win! The material is always there for any student to read and learn if they have the interest or the need.

My plan is to provide an interesting text, making it fun to learn and grow in confidence about your ability to grasp mathematical principles and to learn practical uses for what you're studying. I have tried to write with a little humour and use some real-world examples, like tiling a bathroom or baking a cake. I don't remember ever finding any humour in a textbook. This is my small attempt to redress some of that gap in education literature!

I have occasionally used mnemonics to summarise some elements. They can be useful tools to remember certain rules that you will come across in everyday maths.

I invite students to remain as open-minded as you can and to have a go. Remember to enjoy the journey and don't be afraid to make mistakes. Gandhi once said, 'Freedom is not worth having if it doesn't include the freedom to make mistakes.' So feel free to make lots of mistakes. It's not surgery – no one is going to die and there's nothing to break. In fact, if you lose up to 20% of the available marks, you'll still get a Distinction; lose up to 35% and get a Merit; and even if you lose up to 50%, you still pass the module! Cool or what? (However, I wouldn't recommend this as a study target!) I qualified as an accountant when I was 40 and I was never asked, not once, what marks I got in my finals. So go on, have a go. I know you can do it. I did.

Throughout this book, money examples use the euro symbol (€). Needless to say, the maths holds true for any currency.

I would also like to mention that it is normal to make mistakes, so don't worry if it takes you some time to get things right. While I hope I have not made any mistakes in this book, it can happen. If you find any, please let me know; this will help me and future readers of the book.

'You often learn more by being wrong for the right reason than being right for the wrong reason.'

—Norton Juster

'Mistakes are the bridge between inexperience and wisdom.'

—Phyllis Theroux

Contents

Introduction and Background

Let me begin with a not very sincere apology: the only time I will use the word 'mathematics' in this book is in this sentence. From here on, I'm using the word maths only. OK? If this offends you, feel free to send me an email! Seriously, though, the word scares lots of people who suffered from difficult learning conditions of one sort or another when they were at school. I want you to enjoy this book and this subject.

So why write a book called *Using Business Maths*? Because maths is a valuable, daily life skill, that's why. It's useful and necessary for your personal life, your home life, your work life and for business generally. We use maths all the time, whether you realise it or not: cooking (recipes), shopping (pricing bargains), at the bookies (quite complicated: two to one, six to four, doubles, trebles, etc.) and when following the scoring in snooker (he needs three reds and all the colours to win) or darts (treble 19 and the bull to finish – and remember that finish in darts means to reduce your score to exactly zero, having started at 501). How do they do this? Maths, that's how!

Let me tell you a story about a student I once had; I'll call her Mary. We were learning about adding, subtracting, multiplying and dividing fractions (see Chapter 3)

and I had given the class a question to work on. The solution, as far as Mary had it, finished with the fraction $\frac{42}{2}$. Now you can read this as '42 over 2 or '42 divided by 2'. I asked Mary, 'What's 42 divided by 2?' She answered with a nervous, rushed series of wild guesses: '13? 25? 19?' She was stressed and upset, so I said, 'Whoa, hold on there, you're guessing. What's half of 42?' And quick as a flash, without so much as a moment's hesitation, she said, '21.' Right answer.

You see, as a child she didn't 'get' maths, so she grew to adulthood with the impression that she would never be able to do maths. So when I presented her with a maths problem, her brain said, 'Uh oh, maths. We don't/won't/can't do maths. Panic stations. Guess, for God's sake. G-U-E-S-S. Anything to escape this!' But as you've seen, she knew the answer all along. She knew it immediately and instinctively, without having to think about it. 'Half of 42' is living, ordinary, everyday stuff, but '42 divided by 2' was the dreaded maths and in her mind, she couldn't do it. So I ask you to *stay open*. Don't think that just because you're an adult (or nearly an adult) and it may be years since you were in school that you don't know how to do lots of stuff. You *do*. Just remember Mary and be inspired!

Every day, everywhere we go, we use maths. Every time we spend money and check our change: maths. Compare prices and pack sizes: more maths. Check our pay packet, do the household bills for next week and check the balance (if any!) in the bank: maths again. We play games, bet on horses and use some quite complicated maths.

And sometimes the maths isn't done using numbers: watch the way snooker players work out the angle, speed and weight of a shot or the way soccer players kick a long curved pass that goes right to the feet of a teammate running full speed down the wing. These are maths too, but of a different kind. Sure, we can always check a figure on a calculator, but honestly, who carries a calculator all the time, stuck to their shopping trolley, to the races, on the bus? No one, that's who. So my wish for the readers and students of this text is that you will learn to appreciate the importance of increasing your maths abilities and be better able to operate easily and confidently in your life, with friends and in work. This can only be good for you and your family, good for your community, good for your employer and good for your employment or promotion prospects. So this book is not about modules and exams. Yes, the modules are my guide, but you have reasons that are so much bigger and so much more important than any exam: a better life, a better job, a better and more confident *you*.

ACCURACY AND WHY IT'S IMPORTANT

Sometimes students ask, 'Why the need for such accuracy?' Well, when you collect your wages each week you expect to be paid properly for the right number of hours and at the right rate. You expect that the various taxes (see Chapter 9) will be correctly calculated and correctly deducted. You expect the correct money to show up in your bank account (and not somebody else's) when you go to the ATM. The only way these things happen is by people collecting data accurately, calculating your pay accurately, working out the taxes and other deductions accurately and then, if there's anything left, transferring the correct amount to the proper bank account in the right bank. The bank has to receive that information correctly and make sure it gets to your account as quickly and accurately as possible. You *expect* it to be right.

Think of all the maths and bookkeeping going on behind the scenes. There was a major bank computer failure in Ireland and the UK during the spring of 2012. People didn't get their wages, mortgages and other payments weren't made on time and some people even had no money to buy groceries. When these systems fail or are inaccurate, you will be the first to complain. Also, when businesses trade, buying and selling products and services, they need to be sure they are paying the prices agreed with their suppliers. When they sell, the invoices have to be correct to make sure that they in turn are paid in full by their customers. Not every business 'beeps' their products through a scanner, like at the supermarket. A builder or plumber can't scan the new pipes in your kitchen or 'beep' the 6 hours of their time they spent fixing the leak in your shower. They make up their bills for materials used and hours worked, charging appropriately for each. They can only do this if they know what they themselves paid and how much they must charge you to cover their costs and make a profit. They must also know how to calculate VAT and add this to your bill. And as if this weren't enough, at the end of the month they have to be able to show the taxman how they worked it all out. It's a lot of maths and it all has to be accurate.

We will learn about numbers and how to manipulate them by adding, subtracting, multiplying and dividing in Chapter 3. Most people using this book will probably have the basic skills of addition, subtraction, etc. However, some may not so I have included descriptions of the processes. If you want to, you can just skip over the sections you're happy with until you hit something you need to revise or learn for the first time.

We'll look at wages and the main payroll taxes in Chapter 9 and at keeping an eye on your budget in Chapter 12. We'll also look at measurement and all that goes with it, like distance, area, weight and volume, in Chapter 8, plus lots, lots more. So you see, it's a story about life, a journey, and as I said at the start, it's all maths. And remember, it's much more important than any exam.

'The hardest arithmetic to master is that which allows us to count our blessings.'

—Eric Hoffer

Using a Calculator

Every time you buy a calculator it comes with a set of instructions. In my experience, nobody ever reads them! As this is a book to help you learn, I suggest that if you still have the box or manual for your calculator, *read those instructions*. They are usually quite short and comprise a series of simple calculations and a matching list of the buttons to press to get the right answer for each calculation. You know the saying 'it does what it says on the tin'? Of course you do, but do you read what the tin says? Let's mimic what a typical calculator says on the tin.

My calculator has the following buttons:

Numbers	0 to 9
Plus	+
Minus	−
Multiply	×
Divide	÷
Square root	√
Percentage	%

Change sign	+/−
Add to memory	M+
Deduct from memory	M−
Memory recall	MR
Memory clear	MC
Memory recall and clear	MRC (combining MR and MC)
Equals	=
Clear all	AC
Clear entry	C or CE (sometimes with on/off)

In most cases you punch the buttons in order, like you might speak the calculation.

ADDITION

$$3 + 5 =$$

Speak this out loud and press each button as you say it (except the answer – leave that to the calculator!). And no, it won't speak the answer. 'Three plus five equals' and bingo, your answer is 8.

SUBTRACTION

$$7 − 4 =$$

Say it again, pressing the buttons at the same time: 'Seven minus four equals.' There you have it: your answer is 3.

MULTIPLICATION

$$5 \times 8 =$$

Say 'five by eight equals' (answer: 40). We often leave out the word 'multiplied' and just say 'by'.

One small point here: if you happen to be using the calculator on your computer, then the multiply symbol is an asterisk, sometimes called a star (*). It's 'shift 8' on the keyboard. This is important to know if you're ever using, say, a spreadsheet program.

DIVISION

$$12 \div 3 =$$

Say it: 'Twelve divided by three equals.'

On your calculator, enter 1 2 ÷ 3 = (answer: 4).

SQUARE ROOT

The square root of any number is the number which, multiplied by itself, will give the figure you have. So the square root of 4 is 2 ($2 \times 2 = 4$) and the square root of 9 is 3 ($3 \times 3 = 9$).

The procedure for finding a square root on the calculator is a change from the 'speak it out' system we used above.

What is the square root of 25? Enter the number 25 and press the square root button:

$$25 \sqrt{}$$

The answer appears on the screen as 5.

Try the square root of 144:

$$144 \sqrt{}$$

The answer is 12. (Go on, check it: $12 \times 12 = ?$)

LONGER COMPOUND CALCULATIONS

Longer compound calculations (ones with different operations like add, subtract and multiply) look like this:

$$5 + 6 + 7 - 4 =$$

Enter it as you would speak it: 'Five plus six plus seven minus (or less) four equals.' I got 14 – what did you get? If it wasn't 14, try again. As with using your head for simple calculations, you may have to practise to get confident with the calculator. It's just a tool like any other and you have to learn how to use it.

Try another:

$$6 + 4 - 5 - 2 + 8 =$$

'Six plus four minus five minus two plus eight equals' (answer: 11).

Sometimes you'll get a calculation where the answer is a minus number, like when your bank account is overdrawn because you've spent more money than you had in the bank. You have €65, you top up your phone with €20 and you get €50 from the ATM. Using your calculator, work out the balance.

'Sixty-five minus twenty minus fifty equals.'

$$65 - 20 - 50 = \text{(answer: minus five, written } -5)$$

Calculators differ a little here. Some put the minus sign in front of the 5, as shown above, while others put the minus sign at the left of the display, so it might not be immediately obvious to you – you need to be careful. It might look like this (the brackets indicate the edge of the display):

$$[\quad\quad -5]$$

or like this: $[-\quad\quad 5]$

If you're doing this for the first time, you might take a break here.

Take a Break

OK, so you think I'm crazy – how can 'take a break' be a study skill? Well, if you remember your school days, classes were around 40 minutes long. This has since been proven to be an ideal length of time to study. It then *helps your memory* if you take a short break of 4 or 5 minutes. The material you have been studying gets a chance to find where it belongs in your memory and links with similar stuff. So you remember better if you take *short* breaks. During the break, get away from the book and the desk you're sitting at. Perhaps walk to the bottom of the corridor or to the front door, or even out into the garden. You have time to make a cup of tea or coffee, but not to drink it! Bring it back to your desk with you.

Now quickly revise what you learned before your break. Spend 5 or 10 minutes (max) going back over those exercises, checking that you know each bit. Can you write it down? Can you recite that definition? Can you do that calculation without the book? Or even without the calculator? Then move on to the next bit, starting again where you were before the break.

In addition, each day you sit down to your books, start by revising what you were learning yesterday for 15 or 20 minutes. Start each week by revising what you learned last week for 30 minutes to 1 hour. Finally, each month, spend the first entire study session (e.g. a whole evening) revising the previous month's work. Take this task seriously, writing down your answers or saying them out loud. Then you know that you know what you've learned. This is a powerful affirmation that will make you feel great and confident.

If you do this – revise what you learned during the previous period for each session/each day/each week/each month – you will learn much more efficiently and remember much more and for much longer – hopefully permanently.

PERCENTAGES

Percentage questions come in several forms:

- What is 20% of 45?
- What is 45 plus 20%?

- What is 45 less 20%?
- What percentage is 9 of 45?

Let's take these one at a time. A percentage calculation almost always uses a final percentage sign (%) rather than an equals sign (=).

What is 20% of 45?

We would normally say '20% of 45 = answer', but this doesn't work on a calculator. We have to turn things around a bit. We enter it as follows:

$$45 \times 20\%$$

and this gives the answer (remember, no equals sign!). I got 9 for the answer. What did you get?

What is 45 plus 20%?

On this occasion, it is again as we would speak it: 'forty-five plus twenty per cent' (remember, no equals):

$$45 + 20\%$$

The answer is 54. You can check this because we saw above that 20% of 45 is 9, so 45 plus 20% is 45 + 9, which the calculator, if I need it, tells me is 54.

What is 45 less 20%?

As above, say and enter it: 'forty-five minus twenty per cent':

$$45 - 20\%$$

I got 36 this time. You?

Again, check: 45 − 9 = 36.

What percentage is 9 of 45?

This last percentage is a little different. The question is what percentage is 9 of 45, or what is 9 as a percentage of 45? Say this as 'nine divided by forty-five per cent'. On the calculator you will enter it as:

$$9 \div 45\%$$

Just be careful that you get this the right way round! The answer I got was 20%.

CONSTANT

This function is very important. It's not included in the instructions for all calculators, even though all calculators seem to be able to do it.

As an accountant, bookkeeper or shopkeeper, there are many situations where you need to do the same calculation to lots of numbers. For example, you might need to reduce prices in a shop because there's a sale on, e.g. all prices less 10%.

10% is got by multiplying by 10 and dividing by 100. 10 divided by 100 is 0.1, so to multiply three separate figures by this amount, enter '0.1 multiply multiply the first figure equals'. Then type in 'the second figure equals' and finally 'the third figure equals'.

Try this: Get 10% of 35, 40 and 65.

'Zero point one multiply multiply thirty-five equals' gives the answer 3.5. Now *without pressing any other buttons* (this is important), enter 'forty equals' (the answer is 4) and finally 'sixty-five equals' (the answer is 6.5).

$$0.1 \times \times 35 = 3.5$$

$$40 = 4 \ (\text{i.e. 'constant 10\% of' } 40 = 4)$$

$$65 = 6.5 \ (\text{i.e. 'constant 10\% of' } 65 = 6.5)$$

You should get the same answers. Try it a few times until you're comfortable with it.

If you can't remember which order to do things in, here's a trick I use. I enter the following buttons:

$$2 \times \times 3 = (\text{I know this will give me the answer 6})$$

then I enter

$$4 =$$

and my answer should be 8, because 2 was my constant. If I get 12 (i.e. 3 × 4), then I know that on this calculator I put the constant *after* the double ×. It never happens, but I always make sure anyway, especially if I'm not using my own familiar calculator.

INDICES OR POWERS

Calculate the value of a number raised to a power, like 5^3 (or five cubed, or five multiplied by itself three times):

$$5 \times 5 \times 5 =$$

We could do it the long way by entering the numbers as above, or simply by entering:

$$5 \times = =$$

I got 125. The power 3 requires three buttons after the original number 5: × = =

Try 3^5 (this will need 5 buttons after the 3):

$$3 \times = = = =$$

Notice there are five buttons after the 3: one × and four =. I got 243 for this one.

MEMORY

The memory function is very useful. You can do one part of a calculation and put the answer into the memory, then do another bit and then combine the different elements for a full answer. You can also add or subtract numbers within the memory. Let's try this calculation:

$$(2 \times 3) + (4 \times 3) - 7.5 =$$

Do the first part (2 × 3) and put it into the memory. Then do the second part (4 × 3) and add it to the memory. Finally, enter 7.5 into the memory as a minus number. To get the answer out of the memory, simply press the Recall button. (Don't you sometimes wish you had one of those buttons on the side of your head?)

$$2 \times 3 = 6 \, M+$$

This adds 6 to the memory.

$$4 \times 3 = 12 \, \text{M+}$$

This adds a further 12 to memory.

To finish, enter:

$$7.5 \, \text{M−}$$

This deducts 7.5 from whatever is in the memory already (i.e. 6 + 12, or 18), so 18 − 7.5 = 10.5.

Pressing MR recalls the answer to the screen, where, if you need to, you can continue calculating.

In this example, we could also press Recall after the first two parts to show 18 on the screen and then just enter 'minus seven point five equals' – you would get the same result. Check it. I got 10.5.

It's important to note that you can't slip in and out of memory mode. You have to be a bit structured. So if you have a long combination of calculations to do and some will require the memory, do those bits first and enter them into the memory each time. Then you can recall and proceed with the rest of the calculation.

Say you had to add the following:

125

1,263

17

10% of 13,566

12.5% of 2,500

You must begin with the two percentage calculations because you won't be able to interrupt your addition. Enter the numbers as follows:

$$13566 \times 10\% \, \text{M+}$$
(remember, no equals sign is needed with percentages)

$$2500 \times 12.5\% \, \text{M+}$$

Now you can either press Recall and proceed or continue to add the other numbers into the memory. I prefer to get back on the screen as soon as possible. Press MR (giving the answer so far) and then:

$$+125+1263+17=$$

The answer I got was 3,074.1.

Notice that I started the last part of the calculation with a plus sign. That's because I have just recalled the memory answer to the screen and the machine doesn't know I'm going to continue the same calculation unless I put in that plus sign. It's only a machine, after all!

So just to be sure, let's check this calculation again:

1 3 5 6 6 × 1 0 % M+ (adding the answer 1356.6 into memory)

2 5 0 0 × 1 2.5 % M+ (adding the answer 312.5 into memory)

MR (recalling those two from memory, giving 1,669.1)

+ 1 2 5 + 1 2 6 3 + 1 7 = 3 0 7 4 . 1

Make sure you can do this yourself before continuing.

Remember, until you clear the memory, the total stays in there. Even if you forget to put in that plus sign, you can go back, clear the screen and press Recall again and complete the calculation correctly. It isn't called memory for nothing!

Another helpful feature on some calculators is that they can show that there is an amount in the memory. On my calculator is says 'memory' in tiny letters on the screen. Other calculators will show an M. Check these features on your calculator. Try lots of different calculations to become familiar with it. It's just a tool, so learn to use it well.

Once you're done, clear the memory, ready for another piece of work. If you don't clear the memory, whatever is in there stays and will accept any other figures you add in (with M+) or subtract (with M−). You can get some hairy answers. I trained in the days when any such machine produced a paper printout of the figures entered. This allowed us to check the calculations (tots), but you don't have that luxury. This is why I would always urge you to check all your calculations by repeating them on the calculator, especially if they are at all complicated. It's so easy to press the wrong digit or button and not notice, especially if you're under pressure. When I was training, we had a saying for when we were rushed and got things wrong: 'There's never time to do it right, but always time to do it again.' So work carefully and get things right the first time.

One final point: as I'll say throughout this book, practice helps enormously. As you go through the book learning skills and attempting various tasks, check your answers on the calculator. That way, you learn how to add or subtract, multiply or divide with pencil and paper as well as with the calculator. Practice makes perfect!

You'll notice that there are no questions in this chapter. That's because there are lots of questions throughout the book and you'll get lots of practice if you use the calculator even where you're asked to use your head. Do both, if only just for the practice!

'A man only becomes wise when he begins to calculate the approximate depth of his ignorance.'

—*Gian Carlo Menotti*

'Anyone who has never made a mistake has never tried anything new.'

—*Albert Einstein*

'On a math test: 2 + 2 = ? ... Me: I'll use the calculator just in case.'

—*Unknown*

Brilliant Basics: Getting Numbers to Work for You

We add, subtract, multiply and divide numbers all the time. It's natural to most people, but if you haven't done much of it you can easily forget or just get rusty. Like any skill, 'use it or lose it' applies. Some people just didn't 'get' maths in school, so this chapter starts at the very beginning, explaining the basic processes of arithmetic. Every skill has its basics: pianists practise their scales, athletes practise their techniques in running, jumping, kicking a football or hitting a golf shot. A sales trainer I once had used to say, 'Do the brilliant basics every day.'

DEFINITIONS

Numbers come in different types, although we rarely think of them in this way. Let's look at a few definitions so we all have the language right. This language won't change your life and you won't be required to memorise it (not by me, anyway), but it just means we understand each other more precisely. If I'm to explain things, I better make sure we speak the same language! (Try explaining to a French person how you like your tea when you don't speak French and they don't speak English.) I'll keep to simple, ordinary words as much as I can. You can always refer back to these definitions if you need to as you go along. Most of these terms are used in the FETAC module descriptors for our modules, Business Calculations and Functional Mathematics.

- **Natural numbers** are the ordinary counting numbers we are used to, starting with 1 and continuing to infinity.
- **Digits** are the individual characters we use to write all numbers. There are only 10 of them: 1 2 3 4 5 6 7 8 9 0.

- **Integers**, or **whole numbers**, are all the natural numbers, both positive and negative, and including zero (e.g. 12, 5, 0, −7, −124), excluding decimals and fractions.

- **Rational numbers** are all numbers, including decimals and fractions, that can be accurately expressed as fractions, where the **numerator** (number on top) and **denominator** (number on the bottom) are whole numbers (e.g. 12 ⅘).

- **Irrational numbers** are any numbers that are not rational and therefore cannot be accurately expressed as decimals or fractions. The most widely known irrational number is pi (pronounced 'pie'), which is the circumference of a circle divided by its diameter (see Chapter 8). Pi is commonly written as 3.14, but it can never be accurately written.

Most people using this book will probably already be comfortable with the basic skills of addition, subtraction, etc. However, some may not so I have included descriptions of the processes. If you want to, you can just skip over the sections you're happy with until you hit something you need to revise or learn for the first time.

Your teacher may want to take you directly to the calculator chapter (Chapter 2), as these are so cheap and easy to carry – everybody has one, as they're on mobile phones. That's fine by me, but if you want to use your brain a bit more by doing some of life's simple calculations on the fly, then you might just try some of the following.

ADDITION

Adding is calculating the sum, or total, of two or more numbers. If you're no good at this, I suggest you practise. Like music, maths is simply a skill you can learn. When I was at school, admittedly a long time ago, we all learned our tables, starting with the addition of numbers from 1 to 12 and progressing to multiplication (so I never did master 13 times!). That approach isn't favoured today, but for your own sake and to keep the brain working, use every opportunity to practise even simple maths tasks. Every little helps and you will get better and better.

Here's a simple matrix to help you. Photocopy it or type it, print it small, stick it to one side of a piece of card and keep it in your pocket, bag or wallet. Refer to it often until you know all the combinations comfortably.

	1	2	3	4	5	6	7	8	9	10	11	12
1	2	3	4	5	6	7	8	9	10	11	12	13
2	3	4	5	6	7	8	9	10	11	12	13	14
3	4	5	6	7	8	9	10	11	12	13	14	15
4	5	6	7	8	9	10	11	12	13	14	15	16
5	6	7	8	9	10	11	12	13	14	15	16	17
6	7	8	9	10	11	12	13	14	15	16	17	18
7	8	9	10	11	12	13	14	15	16	17	18	19
8	9	10	11	12	13	14	15	16	17	18	19	20
9	10	11	12	13	14	15	16	17	18	19	20	21
10	11	12	13	14	15	16	17	18	19	20	21	22
11	12	13	14	15	16	17	18	19	20	21	22	23
12	13	14	15	16	17	18	19	20	21	22	23	24

Why do we need to know how to add and subtract anyway, you might ask? Haven't we got calculators? Well, in all home, work and business situations we need to add numbers, e.g. the number of people coming to a party, the ingredients for a cake, the price of a few groceries or the hours we've worked this week. We need to be able to add up the bills we have to pay each week out of our wages or out of the bank account. In everyday life adding isn't just a useful skill, it's a necessary skill, so *learn how to add numbers*. Take your time and don't be embarrassed. You can learn how to add your numbers with practice, over an extended period. Don't expect results in a day, or even a week. Slowly does it. At first you can use your matrix, but try and get away from that as soon as you can. After a while you may find that you start to know the answer in your head even before you find it on the matrix. That's learning with practice.

EXERCISE 3.1

(a) 2 + 4

(b) 2 + 7

(c) 5 + 3

(d) 4 + 3

(e) 6 + 2

(f) 4 + 6

(g) 5 + 6

(h) 6 + 6

(i) 7 + 5

(j) 8 + 3

(k) 6 + 8

(l) 7 + 6

(m) 9 + 4

(n) 7 + 8

(o) 8 + 6

At this point you should be getting the idea. You can check your answers in the answers section at the back of the book or on your calculator.

Now to add bigger numbers. One important element of adding is how we write numbers to do the exercise, since where we place a digit affects its value in the overall number. They would normally look like this:

Thousands	Hundreds	Tens	Units	Decimal point	Tenths	Hundredths
1	2	3	4	.	5	6

This gives an overall picture of how the value of a digit is changed depending on where it appears in a number. More on this later, but for now let's look at a simple addition example.

$$\begin{array}{r} 23 \\ +123 \\ \hline 146 \end{array}$$

You'll notice that, starting from the right, the units (the 3s) are under one another. The tens (the 2s) are also directly under one another. Setting them out this way makes adding much easier. Make this a habit, especially if you do any bookkeeping by hand. Computers do this automatically, but when using paper (remember paper?), you must be tidy. Start from the right and you can't go wrong.

Going back to the example above, 3 + 3 = 6 (being six units), 2 + 2 = 4 (or four tens) and the final 1 is one hundred. So 146 is the answer.

But what about bigger numbers or numbers with higher-value digits that add up to more than 10?

$$\begin{array}{r} 58 \\ +\ 63 \\ \hline 121 \end{array}$$

As before, starting at the right, 8 + 3 = 11 (one unit and one ten). Write down the unit answer. We add the 'ten' to the next column of numbers (the tens).

1 (from the units column) + 5 = 6, and 6 + 6 = 12 (i.e. two tens and one hundred). The 2 is written under the 6, in the column with the other tens, and the hundred is written, on its own, in the hundred column, which is a new column to the left of the tens.

So now you see that the rows increase in value from right to left: ones, tens, hundreds and thousands. You probably already know that ten is really ten ones and one hundred is ten tens. In the same way, a thousand is ten hundreds.

Remember to practise. You might not get it straightaway, but you will. If you ever played a musical instrument, you know that learning a new chord or a new technique sometimes takes a lot of work before you can perform it with ease. It's the same here. It may be simple, but it's not easy – not if you've never done it before – so practise, practise, practise. Try these, then make up your own. You can always check your answers on a calculator.

EXERCISE 3.2

(a)   15 + 28

(b)   38 + 79

(c)   126 + 72

(d)   1,126 + 273

(e)   857 + 1,265

(f)   258 + 65 + 5,687

(g)   654 + 1,268 + 27

SUBTRACTION: THE OTHER SIDE OF THE COIN

If we can add one number to another, we must also be able to take numbers away. This is called **subtraction** – it's where you calculate the difference between two numbers by taking one number away from the other, or if you prefer, reducing one number by another.

So how do we do it? Let's try one. If I have €9 and I give you a fiver (€5), how many euros do I have left? In maths we write it like this:

$$9 - 5 = 4$$

We say this as 'nine minus five equals four'.

If there are ten of us in the house and I leave with my three kids, how many remain behind? Three kids and me is four, so ten minus four equals six. Or in maths form:

$$10 - 4 = 6$$

EXERCISE 3.3

(a) $8 - 3$

(b) $9 - 5$

(c) $12 - 2$

(d) $17 - 4$

(e) $18 - 12$

(f) $17 - 12$

(g) $16 - 11$

(h) $19 - 15$

These are easy enough to 'see' in your head, as they are small numbers. But how do we handle subtracting larger numbers? It hinges on writing them down properly, as before. So if we want to take 56 from 279, that's not so easy, is it? Write it down, making sure to line up the units, tens and hundreds under one another.

$$
\begin{array}{r}
279 \\
-\ 56 \\
\hline
223
\end{array}
$$

If you write them down like this, it's fairly easy to subtract:

Units: 6 from 9 leaves 3

Tens: 5 from 7 leaves 2

Hundreds: Nothing from 2 leaves 2

That was easy, wasn't it? But what if the digits on the bottom – the ones we're subtracting – are bigger than the ones in the top row? There are some different views on how this should be done. This is how I've always done it and it works reliably, every time.

Suppose I want to subtract 48 from 67. Write it down as before, lining up the units and tens.

$$
\begin{array}{r}
67 \\
-48 \\
\hline
19
\end{array}
$$

Beginning from the right, we try to take 8 from 7 but immediately realise there isn't enough in 7 to take away 8. So we 'borrow' 10 from the next column (tens), giving us 17 units. Now take 8 from 17, which leaves 9. Put this in your units column as the first part of the answer.

We then carry forward the 10 we borrowed and add it to the 4 in the tens column, giving us 5 to subtract. Take the 5 on the bottom from 6 on the top line and you get 1. Write that in the tens column and you're done! Check that on the calculator just to satisfy yourself, or for more practice, add the answer, 19, to 48. Try a few on your own.

EXERCISE 3.4

(a)   63 − 34

(b)   92 − 27

(c)   83 − 45

(d)   47 − 29

(e)   31 − 14

(f)   66 − 39

Let's work with a longer number and take 5,548 from 8,632. Begin by writing it out.

$$\begin{array}{r} 8,632 \\ -5,548 \\ \hline 3,084 \end{array}$$

8 (units) from 2 … not enough. Borrow 1 from the tens, making 12 units. 8 from 12 equals 4. Write down the 4.

Carry the 1 we borrowed. 1 and 4 (tens) is 5. 5 from 3 … again, not enough. Don't panic, just repeat the process. Borrow 1.

Now 5 (tens) from 13 leaves 8. Write down the 8.

Carry the 1 (the second 1) and add to the 5 in the hundreds column, giving 6. 6 from 6 leaves zero. Simple. Write that down.

Finally, take 5 (thousands) from 8 to give you 3. Write it down. You're done!

EXERCISE 3.5

(a)   158 − 129

(b)   292 − 195

(c)   1,283 − 856

(d)   1,247 − 255

(e)   26,326 − 16,459

(f)   6,652 − 3,978

(g)   22,444 − 15,657

(h)   239,239 − 89,789

So you see, you borrow from the next highest column when you're short and you repay by carrying forward each time. And it's always just 1 you borrow and repay, borrow and carry forward. So as I keep saying, practise by doing the exercise, but go on practising at home, noticing when you're subtracting numbers in life situations. For example, you need five players for a basketball team, so you need ten players for a match. Oops, there are only eight of us. We're short – 10 minus 8 is 2. That's subtraction. There's twelve of us but only eight sandwiches. We need 12 − 8 = 4 sandwiches from the shop please. Subtraction again! I have 68 cents but that bar of chocolate is 80 cents. Can you give us a lend of … (80 less 68 equals, let's see,

8 from 0, borrow 1, 8 from 10 is 2, carry 1, 7 from 8 is 1, that's 2 units and 1 ten) 12 cents please! Get it? It's subtraction. Notice it, practise it. 'Yes you can!' as US President Obama says.

MULTIPLICATION

For the simpler multiplication of single-digit numbers, use the matrix. Like the addition matrix on page 18, you can photocopy this and keep it in your pocket to use as you gradually become familiar with how it works. Remember, you help yourself learn by saying the figures you read off the matrix: two 3s are 6; three 4s are 12; seven 5s are 35. (By the way, learn to count in fives, it helps with your multiplication: 5, 10, 15, 20, 25, 30, etc.) Keep saying it. Keep learning. 'Yes you can!'

1	2	3	4	5	6	7	8	9	10	11	12
2	4	6	8	10	12	14	16	18	20	22	24
3	6	9	12	15	18	21	24	27	30	33	36
4	8	12	16	20	24	28	32	36	40	44	48
5	10	15	20	25	30	35	40	45	50	55	60
6	12	18	24	30	36	42	48	54	60	66	72
7	14	21	28	35	42	49	56	63	70	77	84
8	16	24	32	40	48	56	64	72	80	88	96
9	18	27	36	45	54	63	72	81	90	99	108
10	20	30	40	50	60	70	80	90	100	110	120
11	22	33	44	55	66	77	88	99	110	121	132
12	24	36	48	60	72	84	96	108	120	132	144

The matrix is limited to small numbers (1 to 12). So how do you multiply *any* number? Just like the subtraction process above, there is a procedure for multiplying that breaks it down into steps. Let's keep it simple to start and try 23 × 4.

$$\begin{array}{r} 23 \\ \times\ 4 \\ \hline 92 \end{array}$$

As always, line the digits up and start on the right. 4 times 3 is 12: write down the 2. You can't write down both the 2 and the 1 because you have to go on to the tens and that 1 will get in the way. A bit like carrying in subtraction, here we have an extra 10 to be carried forward. So remember this one 10 and continue multiplying: four 2s are 8, so add on that 1 from above. Four 2s are 8, plus 1 is 9. Write this down. Done. (You can check this on your calculator.)

EXERCISE 3.6

(a)   23 × 3

(b)   24 × 7

(c)   43 × 5

(d)   127 × 6

(e)   237 × 8

(f)   862 × 9

Moving along, let's be a little braver and try something a little harder. Let's multiply by a bigger number: 456 × 32.

$$
\begin{array}{r}
456 \\
\times \quad 32 \\
\hline
912 \\
13{,}680 \\
\hline
14{,}592
\end{array}
\qquad
\begin{array}{l}
= 456 \times 2 \\
= 456 \times 30
\end{array}
$$

Basically what we do is multiply the 456 by 2 and then separately by 30 and add the two answers together. Check the calculation above: 456 by 2 is 912. What you do then is write down a 0 on the units column on the next line, then proceed as normal, but starting in the tens column. 456 × 3 is 1,368. Tack on that 0 and you get 13,680. Add 912 and 13,680 and the answer is 14,592. Try it yourself before you try the exercises below. Take your time with these. You're in new territory here and making good progress.

EXERCISE 3.7

(a)   23 × 38

(b)   324 × 723

(c)   643 × 562

(d)   1,127 × 65

(e)   3,237 × 875

(f)   3,862 × 629

DIVISION

Division can be done in two ways: short division and long division.

Short division

Short division deals with small, usually single-figure divisors. It's quick and easy as long as you know your simple multiplication and division (the matrix or tables).

Say you want to divide 1,071 by 7. It's not the sort of thing you can do just like that, so we write it down and work it out. Write it like this:

$$7 \overline{)1071}$$

Start with the first number, 1. 7 doesn't divide into it, so proceed to take the next digit along with the first. That makes 10. Divide the 7 into 10. It goes once, with 3 left over. As you learn, it's handy to write in a tiny 3 over and between the 0 and the 7, as shown:

$$7 \overline{)10^{3}71}$$
$$15$$

That 3 is really 300, but as we're working in small values, we say 30. Now divide the 7 into 37. That's 3 (or 30) left from the first division and the 7, the next digit in our number. 7 into 37 goes 5 times (7 × 5 = 35) with 2 remaining. Repeat the process, writing a tiny 2 as shown below, giving us 21. 7 into 21 goes 3 times exactly. And we're done.

$$7 \overline{)1 \ 0 \ ^{3}7 \ ^{2}1}$$
$$1 \ 5 \ 3$$

This is worth practising.

EXERCISE 3.8

(a) 685 ÷ 5

(b) 741 ÷ 3

(c) 1,518 ÷ 6

(d) 2,574 ÷ 3

(e) 2,792 ÷ 8

(f) 2,744 ÷ 7

(g) 12,683 ÷ 11

(h) 30,876 ÷ 12

Long division

Long division is the name given to the process of dividing by larger numbers and it has its own layout. To divide 15,129 by 123, we write it out like this:

$$123 \overline{)1 \ 5 \ 1 \ 2 \ 9}$$

So far it looks like short division. However, as we divide we write the answer *above* the dividend (the number being divided) and work below. We place the first answer digit above the latest digit in the dividend that we're using (in this case, the right-hand 1 of 151). Placing it in this way becomes more important later.

```
               1
         _____
123)1 5 1 2 9
     1 2 3
     _____
       2 8
```

123 won't go into 1 or 15 but 151 will work, as it's bigger than 123. 123 goes once into 151, so write the 1 on the line above, being the first digit of the answer, then write 123, or (1 × 123), below the 151 and subtract, leaving 28.

Now divide 123 into 28. Of course it won't go, so 'bring down' the next available digit, i.e. 2, making 282, which is big enough to work. Divide by 121. At this stage you may have to guess a little, but with practice you'll start to see what's appropriate. 282 divided by 123 is about 2 times with a bit left over. Write the 2 on the answer line. Now multiply the 123 by that 2, giving 246. Subtract 246 from 282, leaving 36.

```
           1 2 3
         _____
123)1 5 1 2 9
     1 2 3
     _____
       2 8 2
       2 4 6
       _____
         3 6 9
         3 6 9
         _____
```

Again, 'bring down' the next digit (as it happens, the last digit, 9). Divide 369 by 123. You can probably see this is 3 times. Write 3 on the answer line, giving 123, and write 369 below the 369 you already have and draw a line underneath. Obviously there is no remainder, so we're done – the answer is 123. However, just to show there is no remainder, I usually put a dash under the line. I'll demonstrate another one of those for you without any comment and you can practise it yourself and then check your answer against mine:

```
             2 4 8 3
           _____
256)6 3 5 6 4 8
     5 1 2
     _____
     1 2 3 6
     1 0 2 4
     _____
       2 1 2 4
       2 0 4 8
       _____
         7 6 8
         7 6 8
         _____
```

EXERCISE 3.9

(a) $1{,}632 \div 24$

(b) $2{,}759 \div 31$

(c) $4{,}384 \div 16$

(d) $20{,}736 \div 27$

(e) $68{,}556 \div 174$

(f) $179{,}705 \div 283$

The final piece of this jigsaw is what to do if we don't get a nice clean ending, as we have in these exercises. What if there's a bit left over? Try this one: divide 345 by 60.

```
              5. 7 5
      60)3 4 5. 0 0
        3 0 0
            4 5 0
            4 2 0
              3 0 0
              3 0 0
                —
```

The first answer digit is 5 (5 × 60 = 300). Deduct this and you have a remainder of 45. Now, we have no more digits in the original number. So just like you would if the 345 was in euro (€345 or €345.00), you can insert zeros after a decimal point without changing the value of the number. Insert a decimal point and one 0 to start with. When you insert a decimal point in your dividend, you insert one in your answer as well and place them directly over each other.

Now you can divide 60 into 450. 7 times will give you 420. Write that down and subtract as normal and continue, inserting zeros, until you complete the division with no remainder or you have enough decimal places to satisfy your requirements. In this example, the answer is 5.75.

If the dividend has decimals in it from the start, just continue as if it wasn't there, except insert the decimal point in your answer, as shown, directly over the decimal point in the original number when you get to it.

But what if there's a decimal in the divisor as well? Now there's a great question. Again, it's easy to deal with. Write down the problem as before, including the decimal points. Now move the decimal point in the divisor to the right, until it's at the end of the digits. Then move the decimal point in the dividend *the same number of places* to the right and proceed as normal.

Let's take figures from the last example: divide 60 by 5.75.

Write them down as usual, then move the decimal point twice so that 5.75 becomes 575.

Do the same to the 60: 60 becomes 600, then 6,000. So we end up dividing 6,000 by 575. This doesn't divide evenly, so stop after three decimal places. (I got 10.434.) I've inserted all the decimal points so you can easily see what it looks like.

Before:

$$5.75 \overline{)60.}$$

After:

$$575. \overline{)6000.}$$

EXERCISE 3.10

(a) $2,190 \div 17$

(b) $7,870 \div 21$

(c) $7,623 \div 18$

(d) $10,500 \div 65$

'The different branches of Arithmetic: Ambition, Distraction, Uglification and Derision.'

—*Lewis Carroll*

'In the arithmetic of love, one plus one equals everything and two minus one equals nothing.'

—*Mignon McLoughlin*

A Little Algebra

Algebra means doing maths without numbers. A more specific definition is the use of letters and symbols to represent numbers and the relationships between them. It allows you to use a formula, a general statement, which can then have numbers applied to it.

Is algebra useful? Of course it is, but sometimes you wonder – until you find a maths problem you need to figure out and algebra is the only way. Here's a simple one:

$$x = 5y$$

This could express how much I sell in my shop in a week. The sales value, x, equals the price, €5, times the number of items we sell. So if I sold 100 items last week, my total sales were:

$$x = 5y$$
$$x = 5 \times 100$$
$$x = €500$$

Let's get some definitions straight early on. Like most subjects, algebra (and maths in general) has a language and if you know the language, it's easier to find your way around.

EXPRESSIONS AND TERMS

An **expression** is a maths statement in algebraic form.

For example, the number of students in a class is:

$$x + y$$

where x is the number of boys and y is the number of girls.

x + y is an **expression** and x and y are **terms** in that expression.

If we know that there are twice as many girls as boys, then we can say 2x = y.

Where this becomes useful is when looking at the whole school or any group within it. If we know that 2x = y, then we can estimate the number of boys or girls in any group, team, choir, etc. If we're planning a trip and the bus takes 30, we will have about 10 boys and 20 girls because 2x = y.

FORMULA (PLURAL: FORMULAE)

You will see in Chapter 8 that the area of a circle is πr^2, or 'pi r squared'. Pi is a Greek letter (it's a symbol) and these are widely used in maths, especially in science. (You've heard of X-rays and gamma rays? They're Greek letters!)

Another simple example is the area of a triangle, for which the formula is 'half the base (b) multiplied by the perpendicular height (h)', or as a formula:

$$\frac{1}{2}bh$$

You'll find other examples of formulae throughout this book.

CONSTANT

Some formulae include a **constant**. Look at the formula above for the triangle. The $\frac{1}{2}$ is a constant; it never changes. However, the b and the h change depending on which triangle we're looking at.

VARIABLE

In the example above, if $\frac{1}{2}$ is a constant, the b and h must be **variables**. They change. Frequently you find texts and teachers using x as the variable. They might also use a letter that reminds us of what we're looking for, like T for time, R for an interest rate or Q for quantity sold. The examples go right through the alphabet and, as I've said, even into the Greek alphabet.

SUBSTITUTION

When you have the formula to start with, you then **substitute** in whatever information you have to help you work it out. Going back to that triangle again: remember the area was $\frac{1}{2}$bh. If you know the base is 4 metres and the height is 5 metres, then you substitute those values for the b and the h in the formula and work it out:

$$\frac{1}{2} \times b \times h$$

$$= \frac{1}{2} \times 4 \times 5$$

$$= 2 \times 5$$

$$= 10 \text{ square metres}$$

EQUATION (=)

An **equation** is a mathematical statement showing that two expressions are equal. We usually have to solve an equation by finding the value of one or more of the variables.

My sales formula at the start of the chapter was an equation:

$$x = 5y$$

If both sides are equal, then if I change one side, I have to make exactly the same change on the other side in order to keep things equal. If you have €5 and I have €5, we're equal. If I double my money to €10, you have to double yours too or we're not equal anymore. How does that look in maths?

If A is my money and B is your money, then:

$$A = B$$

If we double our money, we multiply both sides by 2:

$$2A = 2B$$

If I spend a euro, you better spend a euro too so that we stay equal. Subtract 1 from both sides:

$$2A - 1 = 2B - 1$$

'What's half your money?' asks one of our pals. Divide both sides by 2 — still equal:

$$\frac{2A - 1}{2} = \frac{2B - 1}{2}$$

So you see, whatever we do to one side, we must do to the other to keep things equal.

SOLVING AND SUBJECT

When you **solve** an equation, you find the value of a certain term. To do that you must make that term become the **subject** of the equation. That means it's isolated on the left-hand side of the equals sign. In my sales example, sales, or x, is the subject of the equation. Sometimes you might want to make y the subject.

Suppose you knew that I had made €750 sales in a period. You might want to find out how many units I had sold, which is the y value. Make y the subject of the equation:

$$x = 5y$$

To do this, first turn the equation around:

$$5y = x$$

Then isolate y by dividing both sides by 5:

$$y = \frac{x}{5}$$

Substitute in the total sales figure (€750) and solve for y:

$$y = \frac{750}{5}$$
$$y = 150$$

This tells you that I sold 150 items.

REARRANGING AN EQUATION

Why would you want to rearrange an equation? To try to isolate one of the variables and thereby determine its value. Look what we've just done above – we have rearranged the equation to meet our needs. These rearrangements, or changes, are usually like you've seen: substituting, adding, subtracting, multiplying or dividing.

EXERCISE 4.1

Rearrange these to isolate x (i.e. make x the subject).

(a) $3y = x + 1$

(b) $x + 4y = 16$

(c) $5y = 2x$

(d) $3(x + y) = y + 10$

(e) $3(2x + 3) = (4x + 13)$

SIMULTANEOUS EQUATIONS

Simultaneous equations are where we state a problem in not one, but two equations, both of which are true. A typical example would be:

$$x + y = 5 \quad \text{and} \quad 2x + 3y = 12$$

$$x + y = 5 \quad (1)$$
$$2x + 3y = 12 \quad (2)$$

(A) $\underline{2x + 2y = 10}$

(B) $y = 2$

(C) $x + y = 5$

$x + 2 = 5$

$x = 3$

(D) $2x + 3y = 12$

$6 + 6 = 12 \checkmark$

(A) To solve this, make one term the same in both equations. Multiply line 1 by 2 so you have 2x in both.

(B) Now you can eliminate 2x by subtracting one from the other and solve for x. If you had $-2x$ you would eliminate it by *adding* the two lines, so be careful.

(C) Next, substitute y into either equation and solve for x.

Answer: x = 3, y = 2

(D) Finally, check your answer, as always.

EXERCISE 4.2

Solve the following simultaneous equations.

(a)   x + 3y = 6; 2x − y = 5

(b)   3x + y = 8; x + y = 4

(c)   3x + 2y = 10; x + 2y = 2

(d)   5x − y = 13; 2x + y = 15

(e)   2x + 3y = 10; 3x − y = 4

(f)   −x + y = 6; x + 3y = 6

Solve by substitution

Another way to solve simultaneous equations is by **substitution**. Make one variable the subject of the equation, solve for it and then substitute that answer into the other equation. It's not as awkward as it sounds. Let's try one. In fact, let's use the same example as above (we should get the same answer).

$$x + y = 5$$
$$2x + 3y = 12$$

$$x = 5 - y$$
$$2(5 - y) + 3y = 12$$
$$10 - 2y + 3y = 12$$
$$-2y + 3y = 12 - 10$$
$$y = 2$$
$$x + 2 = 5$$
$$x = 3$$

Proof:

$$6 + 6 = 12 \checkmark$$

First, make x the subject of the equation:

$$x = 5 - y$$

Next, substitute that $(5 - y)$ value for x into the equation and solve for y.

First you get $y = 2$. Substitute *that* into either equation and solve for x. Again, $x = 3$. There you have it. Two methods, same answer. (Whew!)

EXERCISE 4.3
Solve the equations in Exercise 4.2 using the substitution method.

QUADRATIC EQUATIONS

Any equation with a squared variable term is a **quadratic equation**. Usually they take the form of a squared term with a variable, an unsquared variable term and a constant. Oh yeah, one other thing about quadratic equations: they usually equal zero! It does sound odd, but have a look at this:

$$x^2 + 3x + 1 = 0$$

See? A squared term (x^2), an unsquared term $(3x)$ and a constant (1). Or this:

$$x^2 - 6x + 5 = 0$$

Or sometimes you will see this written in general terms, as:

$$ax^2 + bx + c = 0$$

where a, b and c are numbers (called **coefficients**).

The first thing we have to do here is **factorise** these, or find what two factors multiply together to give us these expressions. Oops, language: 'Please sir, what's a factor?'

Stupid Questions

I love 'stupid questions' because there's no such thing to a teacher as a stupid question. Well, actually there is: a stupid question is one that troubles you but you don't ask it. A stupid question is one you have in your head during class when you realise you haven't a clue what the teacher is saying, but you say to yourself, 'I've not been paying attention/I'm 16/I'm a managing director, and therefore I should know this. I won't ask because I'll look stupid.' Believe me, the very best questions are those basic, 'stupid' questions. Next time you have one, say something like this: 'Excuse me, this might be a stupid question, but…' Or another way I offer students is, 'May I ask a stupid question?' Teachers – well, good teachers – love stupid questions!

So, what is a factor? A **factor** of a number is any whole number that divides into it exactly.

First let's remind ourselves about **factors**. Prime numbers don't have factors, just themselves and 1. Other numbers do.

Take the number 24. What are its factors? What numbers multiply together to give 24? Let's look at them:

$$24 \times 1, \quad 12 \times 2, \quad 8 \times 3, \quad 6 \times 4$$

So to answer the question, the factors of 24 are 1, 2, 3, 4, 6, 8, 12 and 24.

Now 4, 6, 8 and 12 also have factors, so maybe they don't belong. The simplest factors, those without factors themselves, are **prime factors**. The prime factors of 24 are 1, 2 and 3.

So where were we? Quadratic equations! Let's have another look at the first equation above and try to factorise it:

$$x^2 + 6x + 5 = 0$$

It's not quite as straightforward as 24, is it? To begin, make spaces for the factors:

$$(\quad) \quad \text{and} \quad (\quad) = 0$$

To give us the x^2 we need, each has to have an x in it:

$$(x \quad) \quad \text{and} \quad (x \quad) = 0$$

Then we need two ordinary numbers which when *added* together will give us 6 and when *multiplied* together will give us 5.

This will be 5 and 1: $5 + 1 = 6$ and $5 \times 1 = 5$.

$$(x \quad 5) \quad \text{and} \quad (x \quad 1) = 0$$

Now we have to figure out which signs connect these terms: plus or minus. Well, there has to be one minus sign to give us a minus in the answer. Try a couple of combinations and see how they work:

$$+5 \text{ plus} -1 \text{ is } +4$$

$$+5 \text{ multiplied by} -1 \text{ is } -5$$

We need 6 and 5. No good.

Try reversing those signs to -5 and $+1$:

$$-5 \text{ plus} +1 \text{ equals } -4$$

$$-5 \text{ multiplied by} +1 \text{ equals } -5$$

Still no good.

But what's left? Try -5 and -1. It seems odd, but hey:

$$-5 \text{ plus} -1 \text{ equals } -6 \text{ (looking good)}$$

$$-5 \text{ multiplied by} -1 \text{ equals } +5$$

Bingo! Correct.

So the complete factors are:

$$(x - 5)(x - 1) = 0$$

Notice that these factors multiply together to give zero. Therefore, one of them *must* be equal to zero because any number multiplied by zero gives zero.

$$\text{If} \quad x - 5 = 0, \quad \text{then} \quad x = 5.$$

$$\text{If} \quad x - 1 = 0, \quad \text{then} \quad x = 1.$$

In other words, you get not one answer, but two. There are always two solutions to a quadratic equation. How crazy is that? Welcome to algebra!

Now check each answer by multiplying it out and see for yourself. Remember, you learn by doing – so do!

EXERCISE 4.4

Find the factors of these quadratic equations. Remember to check your answers.

(a) $x^2 + 3x + 2 = 0$

(b) $x^2 - 6x + 5 = 0$

(c) $x^2 - 8x + 15 = 0$

(d) $x^2 - x - 30 = 0$

(e) $2x^2 - 2x - 4 = 0$

THE QUADRATIC FORMULA

Sometimes there are no easy factors to be found. In this case we resort to the rather awkward **quadratic formula**. This works to solve any equation in the form given above:

$$ax^2 + bx + c = 0$$

$$x = \frac{-b \pm \sqrt{b^2 - 4ac}}{2a}$$

When using this formula, be careful that the equation is in the normal format and then clearly identify a, b and c for yourself.

Try it for a = 2, b = 4 and c = −6.

$$x = \frac{-b \pm \sqrt{b^2 - 4ac}}{2a}$$

$$x = \frac{-4 \pm \sqrt{4^2 - 4 \times 2 \times (-6)}}{2 \times 2}$$

$$x = \frac{-4 \pm \sqrt{16 - (8 \times -6)}}{4}$$

$$x = \frac{-4 \pm \sqrt{16 + 48}}{4}$$

$$x = \frac{-4 \pm \sqrt{64}}{4}$$

$$x = \frac{-4 \pm 8}{4}$$

$$x = -1 \pm 2$$

Solve this using the minus first and then the plus. Remember, there are still two answers, same as above. It can be even more confusing if both use the same integer, one with a plus and one with a minus. Take your time and write all the steps down.

$$x = -1 - 2 = -3$$
$$x = -3$$
$$x = -1 + 2 = 1$$
$$x = +1$$

Finally, to prove your answer, substitute x = 1 into the equation where a = 2, b = 4 and c = −6:

$$ax^2 \ + \ bx \ \ \ \ + \ c \ \ \ = 0$$
$$(2 \times 1) + (4 \times 1) + (-6) = 0$$
$$2 \ \ + \ \ 4 \ \ - \ 6 \ = 0$$

Correct!

EXERCISE 4.5

Repeat Exercise 4.4 using the quadratic formula in each case. Show your workings – the answers will be the same, but you need to show you can do it.

> [**INEQUALITIES**]

What's the opposite of something being equal? Something being unequal. It seems obvious, and so it is. The opposite of an equation is called an **inequality**, i.e. they are *not* equal. That means that one side is either bigger than the other or smaller than the other. (How hard can this be?)

First, some language: there's a whole range of new signs here. Let's look at the various signs and their meaning. Remember, there may be only one way to be equal, but there are lots of ways to be unequal.

$>$ is greater than

$<$ is less than

$\geq$ is equal to or greater than

$\leq$ is equal to or less than

$\neq$ is not equal to

The signs are used as follows:

$6 > 5$: 6 is bigger, or is greater than, 5

$A > B$: A is greater than B

$X < Y$: X is smaller, or less than, Y

Sometimes a number will be equal to or greater than another. For example, your tax bill for the year may be equal to or greater than zero, but it cannot be less than zero. Or a piece of furniture (F) will usually be smaller than the height of the room (R) it is in, but it *can* be the same height (if it's built in!).

$F \leq R$: F is equal to or less than R

$R \geq F$: R is equal to or greater than F

Then there is a simple statement that these values are not equal:

$$R \neq F$$

Generally speaking, inequalities can be manipulated like equations: you can add, subtract, multiply and divide. I say that *generally speaking* things remain unequal, being larger or smaller than before. However, when you multiply by a negative number, you have to reverse the inequality – what was the larger side becomes the smaller side because you've made them negative. This is one of those things that feels awkward at first, but you'll get the hang of it. Check it out:

$$5 > 3$$

5 is obviously greater than 3. But if we multiply both sides by -2, we have to change the sign because now:

$$-10 < -6$$

As I said, it sounds awkward but it becomes obvious once you write it out with simple numbers. And because an inequality also follows the rules, we can still solve for x just like with an equation.

Let's try solving this example:

$$4 - 3x \geq 12 - x$$
$$-3x \geq 12 - 4 - x$$
$$-2x \geq 8$$
$$x \leq -4$$

First take 4 from each side to leave $-3x$ on its own on the left (i.e. make $-3x$ the subject).

Then add x to each side so you have x on the left and only numbers on the right, just like an equation.

Now divide both sides by -2. Remember, when you multiply or divide by a minus number, you change the direction of the inequality. Watch the sign!

EXERCISE 4.6
Solve these inequalities.

(a) $4a > 12$

(b) $2b < 8$

(c) $3x < 18$

(d) $2y + 2 < 6$

(e) $4x - 3 > 9$

(f) $3a - 6 < 2a - 5$

'Men are liars. We'll lie about lying if we have to. I'm an algebra liar — I reckon two good lies make a positive.'

— *Tim Allen*

'We had arrived in an Alice in Wonderland world, at the portals of which stood the Quadratic Equation.'

— *Winston Churchill*

'The human mind has never invented a labour-saving machine to equal algebra.'

— *Unknown*

Bits of Fractions

Your garden's only half the size of ours.
Only three-quarters of the class are here, Miss.
Four-fifths of 12-year-olds have mobile phones.

Fractions are just numbers that can be added, subtracted, multiplied and divided like any others. A fraction is written as one number over another, representing how many parts (top figure, the **numerator**) of the total number of parts (bottom figure, the **denominator**).

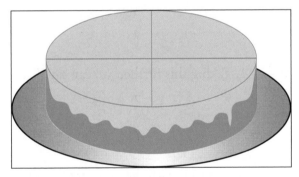

Here's a cake divided into four parts. We know that one of these parts is a quarter. How do we know? Well, just from living every day – from the clock in your kitchen or the watch on your wrist. It's written as 1 over 4, or $\frac{1}{4}$ – that is, one part of four. In this case the whole cake is four parts of four, or $\frac{4}{4}$. Now it's easy to see how $\frac{2}{4}$ is the same as a half, or $\frac{1}{2}$.

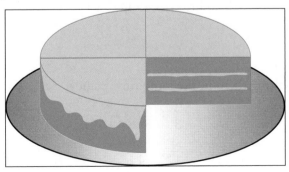

We can also see what three-quarters of the cake above looks like. We write this as 3 over 4, or $\frac{3}{4}$. Looking at this part-circle, we see that it shows three quarters and is missing one quarter. Therefore:

$$\frac{3}{4} + \frac{1}{4} = \frac{4}{4}, \text{ or } 1 \text{ (a whole circle)}$$

Again, if we have all four quarters, we have the whole circle (or cake!). We can see that any fraction showing the same number on the top and bottom is equal to 1. This works for all numbers. We're working from ordinary things we know already towards seeing it and describing it in a mathematical way.

The other lesson here is that we can add the top numbers together as long as the bottom numbers are the same. We have seen from the separate examples above that:

$$\frac{1}{2} + \frac{1}{2}$$
$$= \frac{1+1}{2}$$
$$= \frac{2}{2}$$
$$= 1$$

Also, $\frac{1}{4} + \frac{3}{4} = \frac{4}{4} = 1$. Taking this further, we can say that:

$$\frac{15}{20} + \frac{5}{20} = \frac{20}{20}$$
$$\frac{20}{60} + \frac{40}{60} = \frac{60}{60}$$

When we get fractions like this, with the same denominator (bottom figure), we can combine them as we write. We might say 'fifteen plus five *all over* twenty' and write it:

$$\frac{15+5}{20} = \frac{20}{20} \qquad or \qquad \frac{20+40}{60} = \frac{60}{60}$$

Of course, not all such additions add up exactly to the full $\frac{20}{20}$ or $\frac{60}{60}$. They might add up to, say, $\frac{19}{20}$ or $\frac{52}{60}$.

EXERCISE 5.1

Practise these, writing them in the same way as above.

(a) $\frac{2}{5} + \frac{2}{5}$ (c) $\frac{3}{8} + \frac{4}{8}$ (e) $\frac{12}{15} + \frac{2}{15}$

(b) $\frac{2}{7} + \frac{3}{7}$ (d) $\frac{4}{11} + \frac{5}{11}$ (f) $\frac{3}{17} + \frac{8}{17}$

(g) $\dfrac{3}{15} + \dfrac{4}{15} + \dfrac{5}{15}$ \hspace{2cm} (h) $\dfrac{16}{75} + \dfrac{20}{75} + \dfrac{35}{75}$

As I said above, these are just numbers that we can add and subtract. Try the subtractions in Exercise 5.2.

EXERCISE 5.2

(a) $\dfrac{4}{6} - \dfrac{1}{6}$ \hspace{3cm} (d) $\dfrac{7}{11} - \dfrac{4}{11}$

(b) $\dfrac{7}{8} - \dfrac{3}{8}$ \hspace{3cm} (e) $\dfrac{9}{13} - \dfrac{3}{13}$

(c) $\dfrac{6}{9} - \dfrac{2}{9}$ \hspace{3cm} (f) $\dfrac{12}{15} - \dfrac{9}{15}$

Now try the questions in Exercise 5.3, both adding and subtracting.

EXERCISE 5.3

(a) $\dfrac{16}{27} - \dfrac{9}{27} + \dfrac{2}{27}$ \hspace{1.5cm} (c) $\dfrac{4}{65} + \dfrac{15}{65} - \dfrac{3}{65} + \dfrac{27}{65}$

(b) $\dfrac{28}{56} + \dfrac{7}{56} - \dfrac{16}{56}$ \hspace{1.5cm} (d) $\dfrac{35}{132} + \dfrac{88}{132} - \dfrac{17}{132}$

If we have some halves and some quarters, we can't just add them together. We have to convert each half into quarters (one half equals two quarters) and then add them. So a half plus a quarter is really two quarters plus one quarter = *three* quarters.

Let's translate this into figures:

$$\frac{1}{2} + \frac{1}{4} = \frac{3}{4}$$

$$\frac{2}{4} + \frac{1}{4} = \frac{3}{4}$$

How can we broaden this lesson? Let's look at something familiar: a circle divided up like a clock.

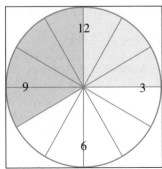

You can see from this clock that it is divided into 12 segments. We have shaded it into different fraction parts:

- From noon to 3 o'clock is three-twelfths, or $\frac{3}{12}$, which you can see is a quarter, or $\frac{1}{4}$, of the circle.
- From 8 to 12 o'clock is four-twelfths, or $\frac{4}{12}$, and is a third, or $\frac{1}{3}$, of the circle. This just leaves us with the unshaded five-twelfths.

Looking at these different parts and describing them in blocks of time, we have 3 hours, 4 hours and 5 hours: 12 in all. Written in fractions, it's:

$$\frac{1}{4} + \frac{1}{3} + \frac{5}{12} = \frac{12}{12}$$

We can't add these easily as they are. If we tried to, we'd get $1 + 1 + 5 = 7$ bits, but those are just odd bits with no meaning. But what if we made them all twelfths? We know they have to add up to 12 because we know there are 12 hours in a full round of the clock. What would the maths look like and how is it done?

We can see from the diagram that a quarter is three segments:

$$\frac{1}{4} = \frac{3}{12}$$

Look at those numbers. We have effectively multiplied the top and the bottom by 3:

$$1 \times 3 = 3$$

$$4 \times 3 = 12$$

Try this with the other fraction:

$$\frac{1}{3} = \frac{4}{12}$$

Careful now – it looks a bit like the one above, doesn't it? But here, to make the one-third into twelfths we need to multiply the top and the bottom by 4:

$$1 \times 4 = 4 \text{ and}$$

$$3 \times 4 = 12, \text{ making } \frac{4}{12}$$

The last piece is already in twelfths: $\frac{5}{12}$.

LOWEST COMMON DENOMINATOR

This shows that we can add (and subtract) any fractions as long as we can get them all represented as fractions with the same denominator. We call this the **common denominator** and we are usually looking for the **lowest common denominator**, defined as the lowest multiple of all the denominators.

Sometimes looking for the common denominator can be tricky, but if you multiply the denominators that will always work, even if it's not the lowest. Let's try a few examples so you get the idea. Like learning any skill, it gets easier with practice.

EXERCISE 5.4

Work out the lowest common denominator of the following and complete the addition or subtraction.

(a) $\frac{1}{4} + \frac{1}{8}$

(b) $\frac{2}{4} + \frac{1}{3}$

(c) $\frac{3}{5} + \frac{1}{4}$

(d) $\frac{2}{3} + \frac{1}{7}$

(e) $\frac{1}{5} + \frac{2}{3} - \frac{1}{2}$

(f) $\frac{3}{7} + \frac{2}{3} - \frac{5}{7} + \frac{12}{21}$

MULTIPLYING FRACTIONS

We said right at the start that we could add, subtract, multiply and divide fractions. So far we've seen how to add and subtract, so how do we multiply and divide? Good news: it's even simpler than adding!

You just multiply the numerators together and then multiply the denominators together. Simple!

$$\frac{1}{4} \times \frac{3}{5}$$

$$= \frac{1 \times 3}{4 \times 5}$$

$$= \frac{3}{20}$$

With whole numbers multiplying produces a bigger answer, but with fractions, the answer is a smaller number! Think about it: the example above is really asking 'what's one-quarter of three-fifths?' Imagine you and a pal bought a raffle ticket for €5.

You paid €3 and your pal put in €2. Now you win the prize of €100. You get €60 and your friend gets €40. Grand. But when you get home, Dad says you have to split it with your three brothers, so each of you ends up with one-quarter of three-fifths. A quarter of your €60 is €15 each.

You now know that one-quarter of three-fifths is €15. To prove it:

$$\frac{3}{5} \times \frac{1}{4}$$

$$= \frac{3}{20}$$

One-twentieth of a €100 prize is €5. Three 5s is €15.

EXERCISE 5.5

(a) $\frac{1}{3} \times \frac{3}{4}$

(b) $\frac{4}{5} \times \frac{7}{8}$

(c) $\frac{2}{3} \times \frac{5}{8}$

(d) $\frac{7}{12} \times \frac{2}{9}$

(e) $\frac{15}{16} \times \frac{12}{17}$

DIVIDING FRACTIONS

This is a little harder, but only because there is a kind of trick involved.

To divide fractions, just turn one upside down (the one you're dividing *by*) and multiply. That's it. Let's reverse the example above so we know what the answer is:

$$\frac{3}{20} \div \frac{1}{4}$$

Turn $\frac{1}{4}$ into $\frac{4}{1}$ and multiply:

$$\frac{3}{20} \times \frac{4}{1} = \frac{12}{20} = (\text{divide top and bottom by 4}) = \frac{3}{5}$$

EXERCISE 5.6

(a) $\frac{2}{3} \div \frac{3}{4}$

(b) $\frac{4}{5} \div \frac{7}{8}$

(c) $\frac{3}{4} \div \frac{2}{5}$

(d) $\frac{7}{8} \div \frac{5}{6}$

MIXED NUMBERS

Mixed numbers are numbers that are part whole numbers and part fractions. Whether you know it or not, you already know them well – and have done since you were very little. 'Sheila is four,' says her mother. 'No I'm not, I'm 4½,' Shelia says. Sheila's 4½ is a mixed number: part whole number, part fraction. So how do we deal with these? We need another new term.

IMPROPER FRACTIONS

We convert our mixed numbers into what are called **improper fractions**. These are fractions where the numerator is bigger than the denominator, making the value more than a whole unit, e.g. $\frac{3}{2}, \frac{7}{5}, \frac{27}{15}$. Before we can manipulate these we must first convert the mixed number to an improper fraction. Let's look at a very simple improper fraction:

$$1½$$

What is this? We already know that $\frac{2}{2} = 1$, so we can add this to the half:

$$\frac{2}{2} + \frac{1}{2} = \frac{3}{2}$$

Another way to describe what we've done is to multiply the whole number by the denominator (bottom) of the fraction and add it to the numerator (top), giving a new, larger numerator. In this case it's:

$$2 \times 1 = 2 + 1 = 3, so \frac{3}{2}$$

Try a few to practise and learn by doing.

EXERCISE 5.7

Convert the following mixed numbers into improper fractions.

(a) 1¾

(b) 2¼

(c) 3½

(d) 7¾

(e) 14⅓

(f) 8⅔

(g) 16⅖

(h) 19⁴⁄₇

EXERCISE 5.8

Using the answers from Exercise 5.7, try these.

(a) a × b   (d) d × f   (g) h ÷ c

(b) d × b   (e) c ÷ a   (h) g ÷ f

(c) a × e   (f) d ÷ b

SIMPLIFYING A FRACTION

Sometimes when trying to solve a fractions problem you'll have a fraction such as $\frac{15}{27}$. I don't know about you, but I'm not able to divide 27 into 15 in my head. But if you examine the figures above and below the line, you see that we can divide both by 3. This gives a much simpler fraction with much easier numbers to work with: $\frac{5}{9}$.

When writing this we show it as follows:

$$\frac{15}{27} \qquad \text{divide by 3 above and below} \quad \frac{\cancel{15}^{\,5}}{\cancel{27}_{\,9}} \quad \text{or} \quad \frac{5}{9}$$

This also works multiple times, so if we had a large pair of numbers as numerator and denominator, we could do this:

$$\frac{\cancel{42}^{\,14}}{\cancel{105}_{\,35}} \quad \text{or} \quad \frac{\cancel{14}^{\,2}}{\cancel{35}_{\,5}} \quad \text{or} \quad \frac{2}{5}$$

We divided above and below, first by 3 and then by 7.

CANCELLING

One last point that makes multiplying fractions even easier – it's called **cancelling**. It's just simplifying on a grander scale. We can cancel figures from the different fractions in the multiplication like this:

$$\frac{4}{5} \times \frac{15}{16} \qquad \text{and using cancelling, simplify}$$

First cancel by dividing 4 into both the 4 (above in the first fraction) and the 16 (below in the second).

$$\frac{\cancel{4}^{\,1}}{5} \times \frac{15}{\cancel{16}_{\,4}}$$

Then cancel again by dividing the 15 above and the 5 below by 5:

$$\frac{\cancel{4}^{1}}{\cancel{5}_{1}} \times \frac{\cancel{15}^{3}}{\cancel{16}_{4}}$$

This leaves us with $\frac{1}{1} \times \frac{3}{4}$, which is $1 \times \frac{3}{4}$, or simply $\frac{3}{4}$.

When multiplying fractions, it helps a lot and speeds up your work if you can cancel/simplify as much as possible before you start any calculating.

SUMMARY

This chapter has a lot of new language, so let's revise the terms.

- **Numerator** is the top number in a fraction.
- **Denominator** is the bottom number in a fraction.
- **Mixed numbers** are made up of whole numbers and fractions.
- **Lowest common denominator** is needed when adding or subtracting fractions where the denominators are different.
- **Improper fractions** are fractions where the top number (numerator) is greater than the bottom number (denominator).
- **Simplifying fractions** is a procedure to reduce the size of numerators and denominators in fractions to make them easier to handle.
- **Cancelling fractions** is a procedure to simplify several fractions prior to multiplying or dividing them.

'Five out of four people have trouble with fractions.'

—*Unknown*

'The margin between success and drama is fractional.'

—*Jacky Ickx*

What's the Point in Decimals?

Money is expressed in decimals. If you can add, subtract, multiply and divide money amounts, then you can do those things with anything expressed in decimals.

  1 euro equals 100 cents

  1 metre equals 100 centimetres

  1 metre also equals 1,000 millimetres

  1 litre equals 1,000 millilitres

Just as amounts greater than zero are counted in tens, hundreds and thousands as they get bigger and bigger, decimals are also measured in tenths, hundredths and thousandths as the parts of a unit get smaller and smaller.

In the decimal world, if you have half of something you have five-tenths of it. This is written as 'point five', or 0.5. We can also add zeros to the right as we do in money, where 50 cents is written as €0.50 or €0.5.

The decimal point separates the whole number from the decimal part. Everything to the left of the decimal point are whole units and everything to the right are parts of a whole, like fractions. Written down, they look like this:

$$1½ = 1.5$$

- .5 is five-tenths, or $\frac{5}{10}$.
- .50 is fifty-hundredths, or $\frac{50}{100}$, which we are used to in money, where we have 50 cents out of a 100-cent euro.
- .500 is 500-thousandths, or $\frac{500}{1,000}$.

We can see that zeros at the end of a decimal don't change its value, as all the above are the same value.

One-hundredth of a euro is 1 cent and 50 cents is half a euro, so .5 and .50 are the same thing – half of whatever unit we are using.

Again, with money we know that a zero after the decimal but *before* a number *does* affect its value. So €0.05 is *not* half a euro – it is 5 cents (or five-hundredths of a euro).

Let's recap. We already know that where a digit is placed in a number determines its value. Looking at the following table, you can see how things fit in a number with decimals added.

Thousands	Hundreds	Tens	Units	Decimal point	Tenths	Hundredths
1	2	3	4	.	5	6

- The 1 is 1,000, a thousand whole units.
- The 2 is 200, two hundred whole units.
- The 3 is 30, thirty whole units.
- The 4 is 4, four whole units.
- Taking these altogether, we have 1,234 whole units.

The whole units are separated from the decimal parts by the decimal point. It's best to keep the decimal points lined up when writing decimal amounts in columns.

The 5 is 0.5, 'point five', or $\frac{5}{10}$ of a unit.

The 6 is 0.06, 'point zero six', or $\frac{6}{100}$ of a unit.

When speaking the numbers, we tend to fully describe the whole numbers and to simply list the decimal digits. The entire amount in the six boxes above, including the decimals, would be spoken as 'one thousand, two hundred and thirty-four *point* five six'. It is *not* correct to say 'point fifty-six'.

EXERCISE 6.1

Write out how you would speak the following numbers as briefly as possible.

(a)   1.50

(b)   12.604

(c)   356.800

(d)   5,678.0765

EXERCISE 6.2

Write the following as numbers with decimals.

(a) Three point four five

(b) Forty-four point zero seven eight

(c) Five hundred and sixty-seven point zero zero five

(d) Twelve hundred and eighty-two point five five zero five

DECIMAL PLACES

We've looked at how one-digit, two-digit and three-digit numbers *after* a decimal point can all be the same value. The secret is that the final digits have to be zeros. So .5, .50 and .500 are all the same value. But sometimes we need to show those zeros so that the numbers look like the others around it. The best and most common example is money. We always show cents with two digits, so half a euro is always written as .50 because we *say* it as 'fifty cents' and not 'point five of a euro'. So €1.50 is not said to be 'one point five euro', but rather, 'one euro fifty cents'.

So how do we describe this in maths terms? We say 'show your answers to two decimal places'. Money is always shown with two decimal places. Many calculators are set to only give answers this way.

But what if the actual answer is something like 2.727? This is three decimal places.

TRUNCATING DECIMALS

The answer is 2.72 on some calculators. They **truncate**, or cut off, the end of the number to leave the required number of decimals.

ROUNDING

The better way to do it is to **round** the number. You can see easily enough that the final 7 is most of a full 10, which would increase the second digit to 3, giving a full answer of 2.73.

The convention is that if the number is 5 or greater the digit should be rounded up, or increased by 1. If the next digit is 1, 2, 3 or 4, it should be truncated. On average, if you are tidying up a list of numbers, you will increase some numbers and reduce others and overall one should cancel the other. (Should!)

If I have to change a whole series of prices for a sale and the boss says to take 30% off everything, this might happen. You fill in the blanks below to two decimal places:

Price €	30% €	Sale price €	Rounded to €	
2.58	0.774	1.806	1.81	Round up
5.52	1.656	3.864	3.86	Truncate
3.65	1.095	2.555		
5.74	1.722	4.018		
9.45	2.835	6.615		
6.86	2.058	4.802		
33.80	10.140	23.660	23.67	

When you're done, check your tot to make sure it agrees with mine. Notice that even a short list like this has a rounding difference of 1 cent (it happens): €23.66 as opposed to €23.67. It will rarely be precisely correct, but 1 cent in €23.66 isn't bad! You'll get it back next time.

Sometimes it will suit to have an answer correct to one decimal place. If you want greater accuracy you'll make it three or four decimal places, but for money, it's always two decimal places. We'll see this as we go through the book, especially in Chapter 8 on measurement.

EXERCISE 6.3

Write the following correct to one decimal place.

(a) 1.35

(b) 1.6386

(c) 1.945

(d) 1.7512

Write the following correct to three decimal places.

(e) 1.35

(f) 1.6386

(g) 1.9495

(h) 1.12548

ADDING DECIMALS

We have seen that decimals are written depending on how accurate you need to be. We now have to look at adding them together – without a calculator. The secret here is to write them down neatly, and the best way to do that is to keep the decimal points below one another. When you get this right, you are left with neat columns of figures where the figures to the left of the decimal point are units, tens and hundreds, as we've already seen. Similarly, the numbers after the decimal point are tenths, hundredths and thousandths.

Let's look at an example:

$$\text{Add} \quad 3.62 + 151.8 + 23.456$$

If we write these carelessly it will look like this and be very difficult to add:

$$3.62$$
$$151.8$$
$$23.456$$

The decimal points are all over the place and nothing is in line. Try it again, but with the decimal points lined up. It also makes things feel a lot easier if you add zeros to the end of the numbers with fewer decimal places, such as the first two numbers here (remember, adding zeros after the last decimal doesn't change the value of the number):

$$
\begin{array}{ll}
3.620 & \text{(3.62 becomes 3.620 by adding one zero)} \\
151.800 & \text{(151.8 becomes 151.800 by adding two zeros)} \\
\underline{23.456} & \\
\underline{178.876} &
\end{array}
$$

Other than getting the neatness right, adding decimals is the same as adding whole numbers. You start from the right and work your way towards the left. You start with the smallest figure and work your way up the values – thousandths, hundredths, tenths, decimal point, units, tens, hundreds, thousands, etc. Just keep the decimal point in its position and work around it as if it didn't exist.

EXERCISE 6.4

Add each of the following.

(a) 0.7 + 0.6

(b) 1.2 + 3.5

(c) 12.34 + 2.65

(d) 35.35 + 45.89

(e) 2.365 + 6.7852 + 8.05

(f) 215 + 46.789 + 0.76

(g) 678.52 + 1.006 + 23.654

SUBTRACTING DECIMALS

No surprises here, just the same procedure as before: keep the decimal points in line, and to make things feel comfortable, add zeros where necessary, then subtract as normal. Now try Exercise 6.5 and 6.6.

EXERCISE 6.5

(a) Take 1.4 from 2.9

(b) Take 12.62 from 25.066

(c) Take 78.034 from 186.5

(d) Take 186.502 from 1,242

EXERCISE 6.6

(a) 0.7 − 0.6

(b) 5.2 − 3.05

(c) 12.34 − 0.65

(d) 35.357 − 25.89

(e) 122 − 6.7852

(f) 563.85 − 125

MULTIPLYING DECIMALS

Tens, hundreds and thousands

At the start of this chapter I talked about the beauty of the metric system and how everything is in tens, hundreds and thousands. This starts to pay dividends when we multiply decimals.

Try multiplying 1.234 by 10. When you get your answer, multiply that by 10. Pay attention to each answer. What do you see? They look similar, don't they? That's the metric system at work!

$$1.234 \times 10 = 12.34$$

$$12.34 \times 10 = 123.4$$

The decimal point is just moved one place to the right each time we multiply by 10. Multiplying again by 10 does it again: the decimal point moves one more place to the right. So multiplying by 100 (that's what 10 × 10 is) moves the decimal point *two* places to the right.

So what if there are no places to move the decimal point to? Simply add zeros.

$12 \times 10 = 120$ (just add one zero)

$23.5 \times 100 = 2,350$ (move the decimal place to the right, then add a zero)

Now try these.

EXERCISE 6.7

Check your answers on a calculator just to be sure.

(a) 123.456×100

(b) 39.0865×100

(c) 123.4×100

(d) $22.56 \times 1,000$

(e) $67.6002 \times 1,000$

(f) $0.032 \times 1,000$

Multiplying decimals by decimals

This is almost exactly the same as multiplying ordinary whole numbers, just like we saw in Chapter 3. Obviously we do have decimal points to deal with, but it's not hard. Have a look at this example:

$$2.3 \times 4.5$$

If this was 23 × 45 we would write them one under the other and multiply like this:

$$
\begin{array}{r}
23 \\
45 \\
\hline
115 \\
920 \\
\hline
1{,}035
\end{array}
$$

So let's insert those decimal points.

$$
\begin{array}{r}
2.3 \\
4.5 \\
\hline
115 \\
920 \\
\hline
1035
\end{array}
$$

We multiply as if there were no decimal points and then count the decimal places in the original numbers. 2.3 has one decimal point and 4.5 has another: that's two decimal places. Now simply count two digits from the right and insert the decimal point.

Working from the right, 5 is one decimal place and 3 is the second, so insert the decimal place after the 3. The answer is 10.35.

As before, the best way to learn this is to try a few on paper first and then check them on the calculator.

EXERCISE 6.8

(a)   3.7 × 2.3

(b)   4.2 × 5.4

(c)   15.32 × 2.1

(d)   23.86 × 34.24

(e)   127.5 × 9.652

(f)   0.052 × 5.6

DIVIDING DECIMALS

Tens, hundreds and thousands

If we can multiply a number by 10, 100 or 1,000 simply by moving the decimal point to the *right*, how do you think we divide? Move the decimal point to the *left*, of course! Let's try a few.

EXERCISE 6.9

(a)   125.6 ÷ 100

(b)   5.9725 ÷ 10

(c)   6,938.72 ÷ 1,000

(d)   258.63 ÷ 100

(e)   36.57 ÷ 100

(f)   1.36 ÷ 1,000

Not hard, is it? You get to realise what this looks like, both for multiplying and dividing, and it can be really useful.

Dividing decimal numbers

Like multiplying, this is similar to dividing by whole numbers but we must learn how to handle the decimal points. This one is a little trickier, but again, it's not difficult.

Let's divide 65 by 2.6.

$$2.6\,\overline{)6\,5}$$

We have a decimal point in the divisor, which messes with the division. To keep things simple, eliminate the decimal point. Multiply by enough tens to get rid of it (i.e. move it to the right until it's at the end of your digits). In this case, just one place does it. Now move the decimal place in the dividend by the same number of places. The decimal point in 65 is after the 5, so just add a zero. The (unseen) decimal point is now after the zero, giving you 650 divided by 26.

$$
\begin{array}{r}
2\ 5 \\
2\ 6\,\overline{)6\ 5\ 0} \\
5\ 2 \\
\hline
1\ 3\ 0 \\
1\ 3\ 0 \\
\hline
\end{array}
$$

But life is never that simple – what if there's a decimal in the dividend? Try dividing 35.4 by 15.

The secret here is to keep your decimal points neatly in a row. When you come to the decimal, put one in your answer directly overhead. Then keep going until you're finished, as if there was no decimal at all. You can virtually ignore it once you get the order right and the decimal point is in the right place.

```
           2. 3 6
   1 5 )3 5. 4
       3 0
         5 4
         4 5
           9 0
           9 0
           ─
```

Ignore the gap between the 5 and 4 of 54 and proceed as normal.

'I believe that economists put decimal points in their forecasts to show they have a sense of humour.'

— *William Gilmore Simms*

Percentages Are Everywhere

Percentages bring together all we've learned in the previous two chapters on fractions and decimals. Percentages are central to any study of business maths.

Percentages are everywhere in business and all through this book:

- Income tax is deducted at 20% and 41% (Chapter 9).
- VAT is charged at 23%, 13.5%, 8% and 0% (Chapter 10).
- Profit is measured as a percentage of sales (Chapter 13).
- Interest rates are quoted as percentages (Chapter 11).
- Commissions are calculated as a percentage of sales (Chapter 9).
- Bonuses are expressed as a percentage of salary.
- Pension contributions are deducted at a percentage rate.

WHAT ARE PERCENTAGES?

The phrase 'per cent' means 'in each hundred'. So if 10% of the students in our school are Polish, then in any group of 100 students, you would expect to find 10 Polish students.

To be a little more formal, **percentages** might be defined as a way of expressing a ratio, fraction or decimal as parts of a hundred. That's $\frac{10}{100}$ or $\frac{1}{10}$, or as we would say it, 'one in ten' or 'ten per cent'.

Percentages are a way of getting awkward numbers into a shape we can understand. 3,695 out of a total of 8,211 might not be very meaningful, but if I say that 45% of students study arts in our local university, it makes more sense.

There are lots of common percentages that are easy to understand and calculate:

- A quarter is one in four, or 25 in every 100, or 25%.
- A half, or one of two, is 50 in every 100, or 50%.

- Three-quarters, or three of every four, is 75 in every 100, or 75%.

- One-third is one in three, or 33⅓ in every 100, or 33.3% (often written as 33%).

- Two-thirds is 66⅔ in every 100, or 66.67% (often written as 66% or sometimes as the more correct 67%).

- One-fifth, or one in five, is 20 in every 100, or 20%. Two-fifths is 40%, three-fifths is 60% and four-fifths is 80%.

- One in eight is 12½%.

- One in 20 is 5%.

ADVANTAGE OF USING PERCENTAGES

Let's say I run a souvenir shop in a busy street in Dublin and you run a small souvenir shop in a rural village. Our businesses are going to look very different. I sell huge numbers of items to the crowds of tourists in the city, while you sell much smaller quantities to your customers. However, if we both express our income and expenses as percentages of sales, then your figures and mine both add up to 100, so we can understand each other. What percentage do you spend on wages, rent, insurance, etc.? We don't need to know the money amounts, just the percentages. Awkward numbers can be simplified.

CONVERTING FRACTIONS TO PERCENTAGES

Let's check a couple of the figures from that list above. To convert a fraction to a percentage, multiply by 100:

$$\text{Quarter:} \frac{1}{4} = \frac{1}{4} \times 100 = \frac{1}{4} \times \frac{100}{1} = \frac{100}{4} = 25\%$$

$$\text{One-eighth:} \frac{1}{8} = \frac{1}{8} \times 100 = \frac{1}{8} \times \frac{100}{1} = \frac{100}{8} = 12.5\%$$

Notice that one-eighth is half of a quarter and 12.5% is half of 25%. As you become more and more comfortable with figures, you'll start to notice things like this more often and it all gets easier and easier. But don't stress, it will come gradually. Try to observe the maths you come across as you go about living: shopping, on holidays, doing DIY, on your payslip.

And remember, not all percentage amounts are 100% or less. If I double my money, I have 200% of my start amount, so watch out!

EXERCISE 7.1

Convert the following fractions to percentages.

(a) $\frac{1}{3}$

(b) $\frac{3}{5}$

(c) $\frac{7}{8}$

(d) $\frac{1}{16}$

(e) $1\frac{3}{7}$

(f) $2\frac{5}{9}$

CONVERTING DECIMALS TO PERCENTAGES

Similar to fractions, to convert decimals to percentages you multiply by 100. Simple.

Convert 1.25 to a percentage:

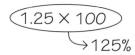

$$1.25 \times 100 \rightarrow 125\%$$

As I said above, notice the numbers here. 1.25 became 125. We just moved the decimal point by *two* places when multiplying by 100. Remember what we saw when multiplying in Chapter 6? To multiply by 10 or 100 or 1,000, move the decimal point the same number of places as you have zeros.

So working the other way, 125% can be written as 1.25.

EXERCISE 7.2

Convert the following decimal numbers to percentages.

(a) .48

(b) .65

(c) .95

(d) 1.34

(e) 2.75

(f) 7.64

(g) 2.22

(h) 12.85

So you see, working with decimals is easy no matter which way you're converting – percentage to decimal or decimal to percentage. You have to work a little harder when converting a percentage back to a fraction.

For example, convert 78% into a fraction.

78% is really $\frac{78}{100}$:

$$\frac{78}{100} = \frac{39}{50}$$

So 78% is expressed in its simplest fraction form as $\frac{39}{50}$.

EXERCISE 7.3

Express the following percentages as fractions or mixed numbers in their simplest form.

(a) 28%   (d) 135%

(b) 37%   (e) 1,100%

(c) 62.5%

EXERCISE 7.4

Convert the following percentages to decimals.

(a) 8.5%   (d) 147%

(b) 45¼%   (e) 1,250%

(c) 67.5%

When pricing goods or calculating VAT, we add a percentage onto a number to give a larger number (a higher price). When there's a sale on we deduct a percentage from a number, thereby reducing the price. Try a few.

EXERCISE 7.5

A shopkeeper has just received a delivery of goods. She asks you to price the following by adding the percentage shown to each item. Show answers to two decimal places (i.e. in euros and cents).

(a) €7.50 + 25%   (d) €13.60 + 75%

(b) €0.85 + 33%   (e) €15.85 + 28.5%

(c) €1.38 + 40%   (f) €53.20 + 9%

EXERCISE 7.6

Add VAT at 23% to the answers for (a) to (f) in Exercise 7.5.

To remove the VAT or the mark-up from the prices shown in the shop, we have to turn the calculations around. This often causes students some trouble. Try using what I call The Model. It works as follows.

As in Exercise 7.6, the prices were calculated by adding 23% to the VAT-exclusive price, as follows:

	The Model	
Sale price	100
Add VAT 23%	23
Ticket price	123

How does this fit with what you have? If you know that the ticket price of an item is €7.50, match it with where it belongs in The Model. Is it (a) the VAT-exclusive price (b) the VAT or (c) the ticket price? It's (c), of course:

The Model		The Problem
(a) Sale price	100	
(b) Add VAT 23%	23	
(c) Ticket price	123	7.50

		Units
7.50	=	123

OK, so our €7.50 is equivalent to 123 units in The Model. Divide 7.50 by 123 to get one unit.

$$\frac{7.50}{123} = 1$$

Finally, multiply by either 23 to get the VAT or by 100 to get the goods value. You get the other value by subtracting. If we multiply by 23, we get:

$$\frac{7.50 \times 23}{123} = €1.40 \text{ (the VAT)}$$

Fill in the blank:

Goods price	?	6.10
VAT	1.40	1.40
Ticket price	€7.50	€7.50

Or multiplying by 100:

$$\frac{7.50 \times 100}{123} = €6.10 \text{ (the goods price)}$$

Goods price	6.10	6.10
VAT	?	1.40
Ticket price	€7.50	€7.50

But not all goods are taxed at 23%. Some are taxed at 13.5% and still others at 8%. We'll learn more about this in Chapter 10.

EXERCISE 7.7

Calculate the VAT at 23%, 13.5% and 8% *and* the respective goods price on the following (i.e. there are three answers for each amount).

(a)   €20.00

(b)   €35.50

(c)   €125.50

If you can master these, you have percentages nailed, and a good bit of VAT too! Again: practise, practise, practise.

'Ninety per cent of politicians give the other ten per cent a bad reputation.'

—*Henry Kissinger*

'Genius is one per cent inspiration and ninety-nine per cent perspiration.'

—*Thomas Edison*

CHAPTER

8

A Space for Area, Volume and Capacity

MEASUREMENT: BACKGROUND AND HISTORY

This chapter deals with how we measure things: length, area, volume, weight, temperature, pressure and even energy.

Measurement happens every day in our lives, whether we notice it or not.

- How far is it to Athlone? (Distance/length)
- What's the limit on this road? (Speed)
- How big is the garden? (Area)
- You're so slim. How much have you lost? (Weight)
- How long does it take to roast a chicken? (Time)
- How hot is it in Spain today? (Heat/temperature)
- How many calories are in that? (Energy)
- How much air do I put in the front tyres? (Pressure)
- How much diesel does the car take? (Volume/capacity)

That's a lot of different measurements, but there's nothing on this list you won't have heard at some time in the last few months, weeks or even days.

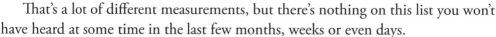
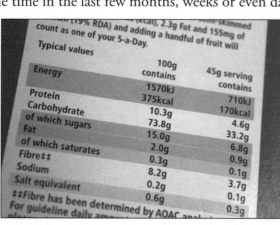

For example, can you tell me how long this line is?

A ⟵————————————————————⟶ B

'Easy,' you say as you reach into your bag for a ruler. But what if I tell you that we're in ancient times and nobody has invented the ruler yet, and that you don't have words like metres, feet or inches? So, tell me again: how long is the line from the tip of arrow A to the tip of arrow B?

Eh … um … Please, don't all shout together!

When I do this exercise in class, whether with young students or with business-people, there's always a period of quiet and a sense of 'what a stupid question' (or maybe stupid teacher!). Then someone will say something vague like 'about half the page', 'about the length of my pen' or 'about the width of this envelope'.

Those are all good enough answers, but can you see what they're doing? They're creating a **standard**, which we can all identify, to describe the length of the line. If we all have the same pages, pens or envelopes, then we can copy this line exactly at home, or in France, or anywhere and we'll all be dealing with the same length: the standard length.

A bit of history about standards

Around the year 1100, a yard was said to be the length of the king's arm. You'll agree that that's a bit vague. And what if you get a taller or smaller king? One might be 8 feet tall, after all.

It became obvious in the 1700s that measurements needed to be more accurate. The Industrial Revolution was underway and businesses needed better standards to conduct good and fair trade as well as measurements for the new gadgets called machines. For example, cloth had to be a known size if it was to be sold and transported over any distance with confidence. Remember, there was no email, and no 'snail mail' either, no text, no fax, no phones and you certainly couldn't check on Twitter, Google or Facebook!

Arising from this, kings and governments in Britain and elsewhere tried to establish a standard. Various efforts were made through the years. However, I was unable to find specifically what a yard measured, if anything. It was inscribed on various metal bars, with one effort involving two similar bars exchanged between the British and the French, each marked with an E and an F, representing the English and French copies.

The French, however, got scientific and attempted, with surprising accuracy, to calculate the distance from the equator to the North Pole along a meridian through Paris. They calculated one-ten millionth of that distance and marked this on their own metal bar, and called it a metre (which was just a little longer than the yard). It was later calculated that they were something like 0.02 millimetres out because of the uneven curvature of the earth – amazingly accurate, considering they didn't have satellites, GPS or infrared lasers with digital readouts! And it all gave rise to the science of metrics, or measurement. Everything is based on the metre. This is what I like about the metric system: it measures something specific. It doesn't matter if the king is tall or short, has big feet or small, is skinny or big boned!

LENGTH

The basic metre was divided up into tenths and the decimal system was born. Tenths were divided again into tenths to give hundredths, and yet again to give thousandths – or to put it in terms of length, **metres**, **centimetres** and **millimetres**, respectively (from the Latin names for ten, hundred and thousand – clever or what?).

- One tenth is a **decimetre** (not in common use)
- One hundredth is a **centimetre**
- One thousandth is a **millimetre**

   Similar names also referred to increasing size:

- 10 metres are a **decametre** (also rarely used)
- 1,000 metres are one **kilometre**

Generally when we're using these measures, all our figures will be in metres or in kilometres. We don't mix them like in the old British imperial system of feet and inches. Because everything is metric, decimals do the trick and allow everything to be expressed in the one unit. Any plumber or carpenter today will quote measurements in millimetres rather than feet or inches. The same applies to weight: us older folks still weigh ourselves in stones and pounds, while our children use kilos (short for kilograms, or 1,000 grams). Your dad or granddad probably has no idea how many kilos he weighs! But more about weight later.

AREA

Area also has its own metric measure. Generally we won't be familiar with it, except for the typical land measure, which is the **hectare**. This is 100 metres by 100 metres (10,000 square metres), or about two football fields side by side. An **are**, therefore, was 100 square metres, or 10 × 10 metres. That's about the floor space of a small urban house. Rural students will probably know that a hectare is just short of 2.5 acres.

THE MAGIC OF WATER IN THE METRIC SYSTEM

Having established a standard for length, other measurements were needed. These were gradually developed based around the most common substance: water. Standards were created for liquids, starting by weighing a **cubic centimetre (cc)** of water. The result was called a **gram**. 1,000 grams was called a **kilogram**, or simply kilo, and 1,000 of these (i.e. a million grams) is a **tonne**.

- 1 million grams is a tonne
- 1 million grams is 1 million cc of water
- 1 million cc is 100 × 100 × 100 centimetres, and 100 centimetres is 1 metre
- So 1 cubic metre of water weighs a tonne

Grams also have their tiny relations too, such as the **milligram** (one-thousandth of a gram, commonly found in medicines). It is written mg for milligram.

Weigh 250cc, 400cc and 1 litre of water, either at home or in the classroom. Then weigh another substance, like 500cc of rice or cooking oil. Discuss the result.

Why do other items weigh differently from water? Why is water ideal as a standard?

Volume/capacity

So 1 kilogram of water is 1,000cc. This handy amount of liquid was called a litre. The formal definition of a **litre** is the cube of one-tenth of a metre.

Smaller parts are again based on the Latin names. The only one in common use is one-thousandth of a litre, called a **millilitre**, or mil, written ml (this is 'm-l' for millilitre and not 'm-one'). This will be familiar to most people, again from medicine bottles. How many times have you seen 'take 5ml once a day' on a cough bottle?

Temperature: Centigrade/Celsius

Going further, water freezes (becomes a solid) and water boils (becomes a gas), as we all know. When these two points were marked on a thermometer and the distance between the marks was divided into 100 parts, or **degrees**, it was called **Centigrade** (meaning 'hundred steps'). Then, in 1948, in order to avoid confusion with a similar word of different meaning in some European languages, the term **Celsius** was adopted, in honour of an 18th-century Swedish astronomer, Anders Celsius, who had invented a similar scale. You'll be familiar with this measure from TV weather forecasts.

Energy

The energy used to heat 1cc of water by 1 degree Celsius is called a **calorie**. Now be careful here, because the slimmer's 'calorie' is actually 1,000 of these, properly called a kilocalorie, or kcal, as seen on food packaging. A **kilocalorie** is the energy needed to heat up 1 litre of water by 1 degree Celsius.

So you see what I mean by the magic of water: it's the connection between length and weight, weight and volume, volume and energy and energy and heat.

WHAT CHANCE IMPERIAL MEASURE?

Given all this science using a common substance like water, what chance does the imperial system have? It has no standard measure, no connection between different systems and even different systems for different uses. For example:

- Miles on land and knots at sea; yards on land and fathoms at sea
- Weights in the jewellery trade (troy) and weights on the high street (avoirdupois)

The divisions within systems aren't very helpful either:

- 12 pence in a shilling, 20 shillings in a pound sterling
- 16 ounces per pound weight, 14 pounds per stone, 2 stones per quarter, 4 quarters per hundredweight and 20 hundredweight per ton
- 12 inches to a foot, 3 feet to a yard, 220 yards to a perch (a what?), 4 perches to a furlong and 8 furlongs to a mile. Incidentally, furlongs are still used in horse races (which is fine as long as some country doesn't get a queen with tiny feet or extra-long arms!).

Volumes, like pints and gallons, are really confusing, so I won't even begin. Ships still travel at speeds measured in knots and the sea's depth is measured in fathoms. Help!

MEASUREMENT — THE MATHS!

There are lots of different measures, with different units for each. Let's try an exercise.

EXERCISE 8.1

In pairs or groups, using a tape measure or metre stick, measure the following six items:

- The desk you're sitting at
- The door of the room
- The opening of the door (nearly but not the same!)
- The window
- The window wall
- The floor

Fill in your measurements here:

Desk	Door	Frame	Window	Wall	Floor

Before you say 'that's a cinch', have a go. Measure carefully and write down your answers in metres, centimetres or millimetres. (Careful: 4,123mm is the same as 412.3cm or 4.123m.)

Now compare your answers with the other groups. I bet there are very few answers that are exactly the same. In fact, I'll go so far as to say that there are no groups with any measurements that are exactly the same as another group. (But maybe that's just my students!) And yet, you were saying 'easy peasy'. Remember the carpenter's advice: 'Measure twice, cut once!' Now perhaps you see that it's not quite as easy as it seemed at first glance.

PERIMETER

The first measurements we want to look at, apart from the length of a room, have to do with the total distance around the edges of a room, or any shape. This is called the **perimeter**. You might measure the perimeter of a room for a tile border or measure the perimeter of a garden for a path or a wall. You need to know how many blocks to buy, and for that you need to know the overall length of the perimeter.

The process is simple: you measure the edges and add the lengths together. We can shorten the task if we know it's a square garden by just measuring one side. We know the other sides are the same length, so just multiply by 4.

Or if it's a rectangle, just measure one long side and one short side and multiply by 2.

The opposite sides of the rectangle are equal, so just add twice the length of the two different sides to give the total perimeter (because A = C and B = D): A × 2 and B × 2.

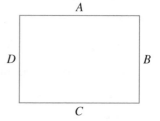

It's the same with a triangle, or indeed any shape: just add the lengths of the sides together to give the length of the perimeter.

Some rooms or spaces are a mix of shapes, with bits added and bits taken out. My family room, for example, has an alcove added onto the ordinary rectangle of the room, but it also has a fireplace, which takes a rectangle away from the floor space. In a case like this, the perimeter will be slightly different depending on whether you are looking at the walls or at the floor. The fireplace reduces the floor but not the walls.

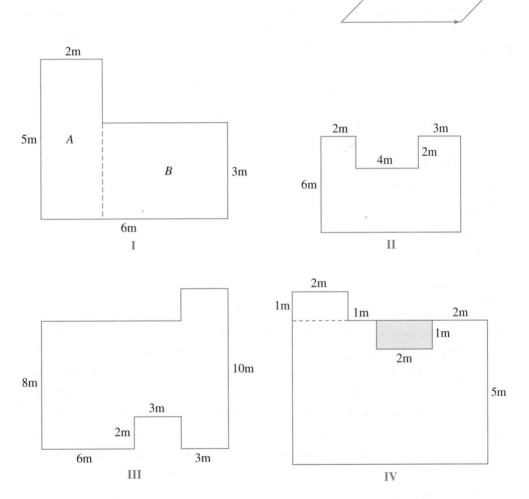

Let's calculate the perimeter of room I. It's a simple L-shaped room. To calculate the perimeter, we can of course measure all the walls. You can also draw the floor plan, measure four walls and calculate the other two easily.

It's a complex shape, but it's pretty obvious that this room is easily divided into two rectangles (A and B) using what we call construction lines. All these problems are much easier to answer when you label the different segments clearly with letters, like I've done.

Rectangle A is simple: it's 5 × 2. That's two walls. Then there's the top wall of B and the short wall of A. These need a little thought. If the entire bottom wall of the whole room measures 6 metres but rectangle A is occupying 2 metres of it, then there are 4 metres left as the bottom/top length of B. This means B measures 4 × 3.

Finally, the height of the whole room is 5 metres, but rectangle B occupies 3 metres of that. Therefore, the short wall is 2 metres. Write in your wall lengths, which now read (clockwise from the top) 2, 2, 4, 3, 6 and 5 metres. Adding these, the perimeter is:

$$2 + 2 + 4 + 3 + 6 + 5 = 22 \text{ metres long}$$

We'll have another look at this room later and work out the area.

EXERCISE 8.2

Calculate the perimeter of each of the rooms.

(a)   Room II

(b)   Room III

(c)   Room IV

AREA

We need to calculate **area** too. Why? Well, to buy carpet or curtains, to fit tiles in the bathroom or to paint the walls of the sitting room. For this we need to understand the shapes we encounter every day. Many are regular, others are mixed shapes and many more are purely random. Let's deal with the common shapes. Notice how much we already know, even without realising it. We know squares have equal sides – it's almost instinctive. Same with rectangles: we know the opposite sides are equal. Check out your bedroom. You know that if you measure one wall, the opposite one is likely to be the same length (unless your house was built by a cowboy – it happens!).

Squares

A square is a quadrilateral (four-sided figure) where all sides are equal and all angles are right angles (90 degrees).

If this square is 2 metres by 2 metres, it has two rows with two 1-metre-square tiles each. We can count them (1, 2, 3, 4) or simply multiply the length by the breadth, i.e. $2 \times 2 = 4$ square metres. Square metres is usually written m^2.

$$2m \times 2m = 4m^2$$

When you multiply metres by metres, as here, your answer is m^2, or **square metres**. When you multiply metres by metres by metres (i.e. three times), your answer will be m^3, or **metres cubed**, and so on. But more of this later.

Rectangles

Rectangles are like squares. After all, every square is a **rectangle**, which is defined as a quadrilateral where opposite sides are equal and all angles are right angles.

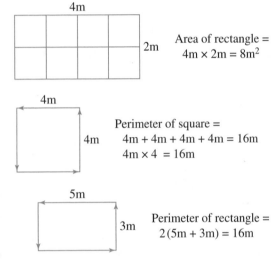

Area of rectangle =
4m x 2m = 8m^2

Perimeter of square =
4m + 4m + 4m + 4m = 16m
4m x 4 = 16m

Perimeter of rectangle =
2(5m + 3m) = 16m

You can see that this rectangle has two rows of four 1-metre squares each, making its area $4 \times 2 = 8$ square metres (8m^2). Whatever the shape of a room, you can usually split it into some rectangles first, as most rooms in most houses are rectangles and have more rectangles stuck on or taken away. In my house, there's a bedroom with a rectangle taken from it in the corner. If you go into the next room, you'll see that there's a built-in wardrobe there. There's another bit missing from the bathroom (the hot press). Have a look around your house and notice these shapes in rooms that are not neat rectangles. Does the sitting room have an alcove or a bay window added to the basic rectangle? Bay windows are sometimes rectangles and sometimes a curve, probably less than a half circle. If you want to buy a carpet for these rooms, you'd better include the alcove or the window!

Whenever you're looking at a room it's always best to draw the shape of it onto a page, even roughly. Measure the walls or the floor and note the measurements on your drawing. You might also draw some construction lines to identify the working shapes and to avoid confusion. Another thing I always recommend is that you label or name each shape on your drawing, usually A, B, C, etc. Then you can identify each separate bit and refer to it easily and accurately. You saw what I did above with room I, II, III and IV. These are called roman numerals.

Let's do another one.

Let's assume this room is 10 metres square. That's 10 metres by 10 metres. We want to put a nice broad border round the walls – let's say we want it 1 metre wide, all the way round. What is the area of the border?

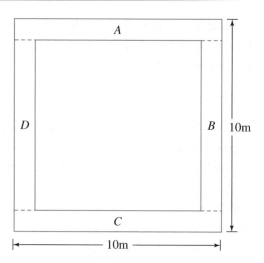

As I've said already, break the shape into parts to make it easier to work with. There are a couple of ways to do this. One way is to work out the area of the whole room, then work out the area of the floor inside the border and take one from the other to leave the area of the border. Let's try it.

First, measure the walls and mark the results on your drawing. We know they're 10m × 10m. Now draw in the border and work out the length of the sides of the inside space – it's not 9m! Be careful.

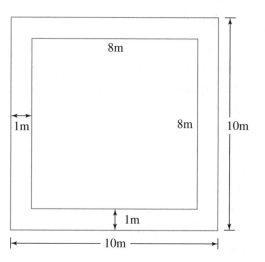

Can you see? It's 8m because there's a 1m border on each side of the room.

Area of whole room: 10m × 10m = 100m²

Area inside border: 8m × 8m = 64m²

Take one from the other: 100m − 64m = 36m²

The other way to do this is to focus on the border, which, after all, is just a series of long rectangles. Draw in the construction lines and work out the sides of the rectangles. Be careful again, as the rectangles may not all be the same length.

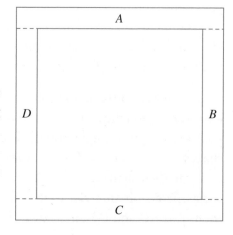

I've inserted some construction lines to make four long, skinny rectangles (A, B, C and D). Look carefully and see where I got their dimensions. I've made two pairs of equal rectangles. Rectangles A and C at the top and bottom are both the full 10m wide and, of course, 1m deep.

$$10m \times 1m \times 2 = 20m^2$$

Rectangles B and D at the sides are both 8m long by 1m deep. They're 8m because the whole square is 10m long, but with 1m off each end, this leaves just 8m each for this second pair.

$$8m \times 1m \times 2 = 16m^2$$

Add the two pairs:

$$20m + 16m = 36m^2$$

It's the same answer as before, of course.

The important point here is that you can solve this problem one way and I can do it a different way and we both get the same answer. The answer is more important than which method you choose. Very rarely do you encounter a problem in maths, as in life, with just one solution. There's always another way, although sometimes you can't see it until you move from where you're standing.

Let's try another example, this time not so simple. Have a go on your own, then I'll explain how I do it.

What's the area of this L-shaped room and of its border (which is 1m wide all round)?

Calculate the area of the L-shaped room and the area of the 1m-wide border. You can immediately see that you don't have all the measurements, but they're easy to work out on your drawing (you have done a drawing, haven't you?).

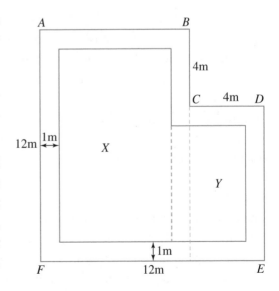

If it was a full square room, the top wall would be 12m, same as EF along the bottom. But CD is 4m, so AB must be 8m. Now draw a construction line down the middle of the room from top to bottom to give two rectangles, X and Y.

$$\text{Area of X: 8m} \times \text{12m} = \text{96m}^2$$

If the side wall, AF, is 12m and the wall opposite it, BC, is 4m, then DE must be 8m, just like AB.

$$\text{Area of Y: 4m} \times \text{8m} = \text{32m}^2$$

So the area of the whole room is 96m + 32m = 128m².

Now do the same steps for the area inside the border. Do it yourself and see if you get the same answer as I do. Again, be careful with your construction line – it's not the same line as for the whole room.

The area of inside X	60m
The area of inside Y	24m
Adding, we get:	84m²
Whole room	128m²
Less inside space	84m
Area of the border	44m²

Doing the drawing and construction lines and working out the missing bits of information are useful because sometimes you can't measure all the walls. Imagine a kitchen with lots of built-in presses and spaces for the sink, washing machine, fridge, etc., or a bedroom with a bed or wardrobe. Again, I'm trying to show you how these techniques are really useful to you outside the classroom. So the next time you find yourself asking, 'Am I bothered? Do I care? Do I want to learn this stuff?', just look for the uses outside school or college – I hope you'll say, 'Yes, this is worth learning and useful for me.'

Triangles

The area of a triangle is easy to calculate once you know the simple formula. Take a page from a copybook or pad. It's a rectangle, either A4 or foolscap. Fold it carefully from corner to corner and mark along the fold with a pencil.

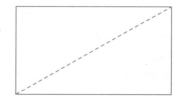

Straightaway you'll notice that you have divided the rectangle into two triangles and that each of these is half the whole sheet. In fact, if you cut along your dotted line and swivel one triangle, the two fit together perfectly.

The area of the rectangle is length by width. Therefore, the area of our triangle is half the length by width. When talking about triangles we don't say length or width, we say the base and the perpendicular height.

In this example, the perpendicular height is simply the width of the paper because the corners are right angles (90 degrees, or square). You might not be familiar with the word 'perpendicular', but believe me, you know what it is! Did you ever see a bus stop, lamppost or a picture on the sitting room wall that just wasn't straight? Well, straight in that sense is **perpendicular**. It means 90 degrees, or at right angles, to the ground or floor. So now you know the maths word for straight: perpendicular.

The formula for the area of a triangle is:

$$\frac{1}{2} b \times h$$

Half the base by the perpendicular height of the triangle, even if the triangle does not include the right angle itself. Look at the following and calculate the area.

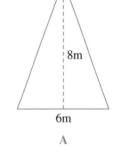

The base of triangle A is 6m. The area is:

$$\frac{1}{2} b \times h$$

$$= \left(\frac{1}{2} \times 6\right) \times 8$$

$$= 3 \times 8$$

$$= 24m^2$$

Triangle B has a base of 8m and a height of 5m, so the area is:

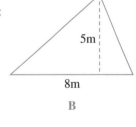

$$\frac{1}{2} b \times h$$

$$= \left(\frac{1}{2} \times 8\right) \times 5$$

$$= 4 \times 5$$

$$= 20m^2$$

Triangle C is a funny-looking one. It's called an **oblique triangle** and the perpendicular construction line falls outside the triangle. Otherwise it's just another triangle.

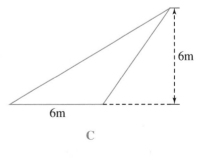

$$\frac{1}{2} b \times h$$

$$= \left(\frac{1}{2} \times 6\right) \times 6$$

$$= 3 \times 6$$

$$= 18m^2$$

EXERCISE 8.3

Calculate the area of the following shapes. All measurements are in metres.

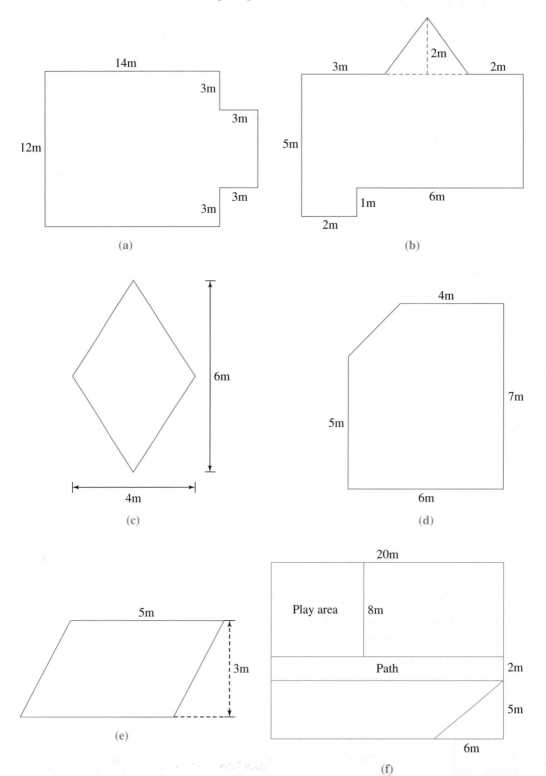

(a)

(b)

(c)

(d)

(e)

(f)

(f) Find the following:

    (i)   The area of the whole park (diagram f)

    (ii)   The area of the square play area

    (iii) The area of the long path

    (iv) The area of the triangular flowerbed

    (v)   How much space is left for grass?

THE THREE Cs: CIRCLES, CYLINDERS AND CONES

It's funny to read a scientific definition of something you're utterly familiar with, like a circle. It sounds odd, like this: 'A **circle** is a flat curve where every point on its edge is the same distance from a fixed point, called the centre.' See what I mean? 'A flat curve' – who'd've thunk?

But it does remind you of a few simple truths: a circle is flat and we know every point is the same distance from the centre. Let's begin with some definitions.

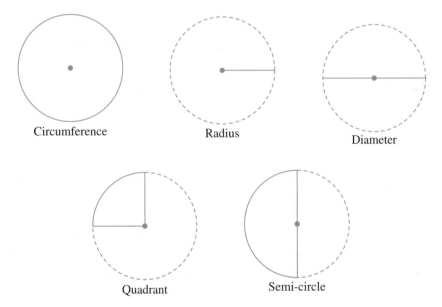

    Circumference   Radius   Diameter

          Quadrant   Semi-circle

- **Circumference:** The total distance around the edge of a circle.
- **Radius:** The distance from the centre to the edge of a circle.
- **Diameter:** The distance along a straight line, from edge to edge of a circle, through the centre.
- **Quadrant:** One-quarter of a circle.
- **Semi-circle:** Half a circle.

Our main task from the maths point of view is to be aware of and to be able to calculate the circumference of a circle and the area of a circle. Some bright mathematician, long since forgotten, discovered that for every circle, the relationship between the circumference and the diameter is a constant – it never changes. It's called pi and is written π. The Babylonians knew pi over 4,000 years ago. In fact, even today it has never been perfectly calculated because it's an irrational number. It's frequently written as 3.14159, but for our purposes it's taken as 3.14.

CALCULATE THE CIRCUMFERENCE OF A CIRCLE

To calculate the circumference of any circle, you only need one measurement: the diameter, or shorter still, the radius (half the diameter). For all the other shapes we've looked at so far, we've needed two dimensions (measurements), but it's just one for circles. Be careful to always check, in every question, whether you are given the diameter or the radius. The formula uses the radius – make sure you do too! The circumference of a circle is $2\pi r$, so try the exercise using that simple formula.

EXERCISE 8.4

Calculate the circumference of circles with the following dimensions correct to two decimal places.

(a) Radius 6 metres

(b) Radius 4.5 metres

(c) Diameter 4 metres

(d) Diameter 7 metres

(e) Radius 15 centimetres

(f) Diameter 23 millimetres

CALCULATE THE AREA OF A CIRCLE

The area of a circle is pi times r^2. This is usually written like this:

$$\pi r^2$$

It means $\pi \times r^2$.

If your radius is 4, then the area of the circle is:

$$\pi \times r^2$$

$$= 3.14 \times 4 \times 4$$

$$= 50.24$$

EXERCISE 8.5

Calculate the area of the circles (a) to (f) in Exercise 8.4.

Let's see what use, if any, this particular bit of maths is to us. Well, if you want to build a pond in your garden, you'll need to know how many bricks you'll have to buy to build the surround. That's the circumference. Same if you want to plant some flowers to make it look pretty. The gardening book says one plant every 15cm, so how many daisies do you need to buy? If your oil tank is looking a bit rusty and you want to paint it, you need to work out the area, and if one end is round, that's a circle. We'll come across this again in the next section.

VOLUME

Volume is the amount of space occupied by a three-dimensional object. We're going to focus on regular objects like cubes and cylinders, spheres and cones.

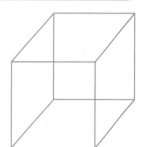

A **cube** is a solid object contained by six equal squares. You'll know a cube of sugar or the Rubik's Cube.

A cube stands on a square. All sides are the same length. Let's say this cube has sides 2m long. The base is $2m \times 2m = 4m^2$.

Now imagine a cube standing on each square metre, making a layer of four cubes. Now stack another layer on top, making a total of eight cubes, each $1m \times 1m \times 1m$, or $1m^3$.

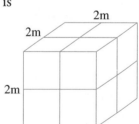

Volume of cube = $2m \times 2m \times 2m = 8m^3$

Notice the tiny ^{3} there. This means that we have multiplied metres by metres by metres, length by width by height, to give volume in cubic metres.

Now if we take a solid standing on a rectangle, like a shoebox, you call this object a **cuboid**. It's just like a cube except it has sides of differing lengths. Your typical shoebox is about 40cm long, 15cm wide and perhaps 12cm high. What's the volume of the shoebox?

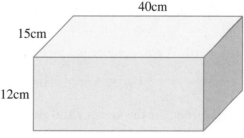

Cuboid = $40cm \times 15cm \times 12cm = 7,200cm^3$

$$Volume\ (V) = L \times W \times H$$
$$= 40cm \times 15cm \times 12cm$$
$$= 7,200cm^3$$

But that's the same shape as a fridge, say, or a kitchen press or a garden shed. Just because something is huge or very tiny doesn't mean we can forget the basic rules of maths!

EXERCISE 8.6

Calculate the volume of the following using length $\times$ width $\times$ height (LWH).

(a) A cube of side 6cm

(b) A cube with 3m sides

(c) A cuboid: L 2m, W 3m, H 4m

(d) A cuboid: L 10m, W 12m, H $\frac{1}{2}$m

On a practical note, I've noticed that when you buy a piece of kitchen equipment, like a fridge or a cooker, they always give the dimensions on the pack and in the user manual. It's normally given as H, W and D, or height, width and depth (out from the wall). What you call it depends on your point of view and preference. What's important is that you understand the maths. The purpose of those measurements on the box is so that you can check before you buy that the washing machine isn't too tall to fit under your worktop, too deep, so it won't stick out into the room, or too wide so that it won't fit between the wall and the press.

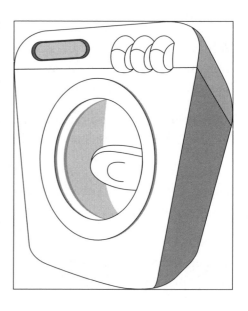

CUBIC METRES, CUBIC CENTIMETRES AND LITRES

Now let's get a sense of the relationship between cubic metres and cubic centimetres. Remember, there are 100 centimetres in 1 metre. A **cubic metre** is a metre by a metre by a metre.

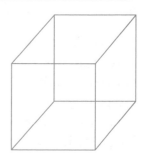

$$1m \times 1m \times 1m = 1m^3$$

If 1 metre is the same as 100 centimetres, then:

$$100cm \times 100cm \times 100cm = 1,000,000cc$$

So 1 cubic metre is 1,000,000cc.

A good check here is to count the zeros – there are six zeros before and after the equals sign. That's 1 million cubic centimetres.

Now notice that cubic centimetre is frequently shortened to cc, as you'll have heard in the description of a car engine (e.g. 1500cc).

CAPACITY

When a shape looks like a solid but is actually capable of holding, say, a liquid, we don't talk about its volume, but about its capacity. **Capacity** is how much material an object holds.

Suppose this cube is smaller than the one above. Say it's only 10cm × 10cm × 10cm – that's small enough to hold in one hand.

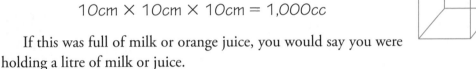

$$10cm \times 10cm \times 10cm = 1,000cc$$

If this was full of milk or orange juice, you would say you were holding a litre of milk or juice.

$$1,000cc = 1 \text{ litre}$$

A **litre** is defined as the cube of one-tenth of a metre.

That litre carton is:

$$10cm \times 10cm \times 10cm = 1,000cm^2, \text{ or } cc$$

So what volume/capacity would a cube 10 cartons long be? That's 1m in length and width and height (the carton is a litre, or one-tenth of a metre, like it says in the definition). Would it be 10 × 10 × 10 litres?

$$10 \text{ cartons} \times 10 \text{ cartons} \times 10 \text{ cartons} = 1,000 \text{ litres, or}$$

$$1m \times 1m \times 1m = 1m^3$$

That's a lot in a few short pages. Let's recap:

- A cube stands on a square and a cuboid on a rectangle
- 1 metre is 100 centimetres
- 1 cubic metre, therefore, is 100cm × 100cm × 100cm = 1 million cc
- 1 litre is 10cm × 10cm × 10cm = 1,000cc
- 1,000 litres = 1 cubic metre

We'll come back to some of this a little further on.

EXERCISE 8.7

Calculate the volume of the following cuboids. Pay particular attention to how you write the units in your answer.

(a)   12cm × 5cm × 20cm

(b)   1m × 6m × 15m

(c)   25m × 5m × 75cm

(d)   1m × 2.5m × 900mm

(e)   17cm × 185mm × 26cm

(f)   28cm × 0.5m × 100mm

CYLINDERS

We've seen that the volume of cubes and cuboids is calculated by multiplying the area of the base by the height: (L × B) × H. We've also represented these solids as layers of cubes because they are evenly wide all the way to the top. This means that if the first layer has four cubes, the top layer has four cubes.

What about another solid, also even all the way to the top, but with a circular base? This is a uniform solid. A uniform solid based on a circle is a **cylinder** – your typical tin can shape, or tank or pipe.

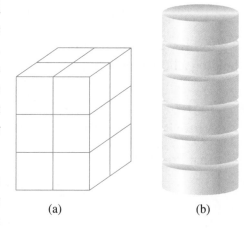

(a)   (b)

Just like the cuboid, the volume is the area of the base (a circle, so it's πr^2) multiplied by the height. Putting that together, we describe the volume of a cylinder as:

$$\pi r^2 h$$

EXERCISE 8.8

Calculate the volume of the following cylinders.

(a)   Radius 2m, height 3m

(b)   Oil tank length 3m and diameter 1.5m

(c)   Garden pond 2.5m across and depth 0.5m

(d)   20 metres of pipe, 4 centimetres wide

(e) How big is the entire cylinder shown here?

(f) How big is the hole through the middle with a diameter of 2m?

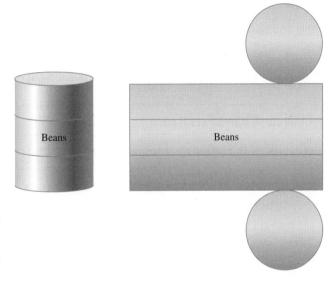

2m

6m

8m

Surface area

Another problem for us with cylinders is finding the surface area. Obviously the top and bottom are circles and we know that the area of the circles is $\pi r^2 \times 2$.

But what about the sides of a cylinder? Imagine you remove the top and bottom of a tin can. What's left? A tube. Now imagine that you cut the tube from top to bottom so that you can flatten it. Look at the drawing – it's a rectangle.

Beans

Beans

Have a good look at this rectangle and the tube it was. The width of the rectangle is the circumference of the tube (the circumference of the two circles, top and bottom) and the length of the rectangle is the height of the tube.

The circumference of the can is $2\pi r$ (which I always see as the same three characters as the area formula (πr^2), just rearranged on the page). So if the circumference is $2\pi r$ and the height is h, then the area of the 'sides' of the can is:

$$2\pi rh$$

This will make sense if we do an example.

Imagine a can of beans with a diameter of 7.5cm and a height of 11cm. In fact, you can probably do better than imagine: take a can of beans or spaghetti hoops out of your kitchen press. Now you can see what I'm getting at here. The top and bottom are two circles, so the area is:

$$2 \times \pi r^2$$

$$= 2 \times 3.14 \times (3.5 \times 3.5)$$

$$= 76.93 cm^2$$

The area of the sides is the circumference by the height. That's:

$$2\pi r \times h$$
$$= 2 \times 3.14 \times 3.5 \times 11$$
$$= 241.78cm^2$$

So the total is:

$$76.93cm^2 + 241.78cm^2 = 318.71cm^2$$

EXERCISE 8.9

Find the surface area of the following.

(a)   A mineral can with a diameter of 7cm and a height of 12cm

(b)   A tank with a radius of 500mm and a length of 2m

CONES AND SPHERES

Let's look at the volume of solids related to cylinders: cones and spheres.

* A **cone** is a pyramid whose base is a circle.
* A **sphere** is a perfectly round solid, every point on the surface of which is the same distance (r) from the centre.

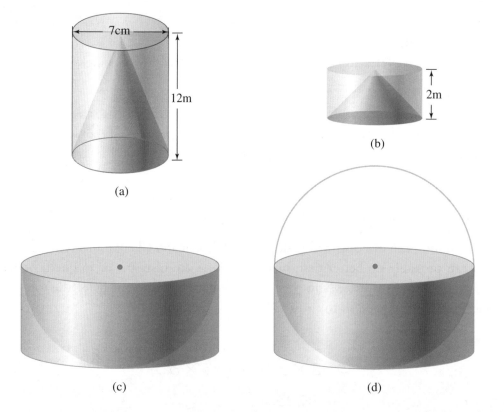

(a)

(b)

(c)

(d)

Cone (a and b)

The formula for the volume of a cone is one-third of that of a cylinder:

$$\frac{1}{3}(\pi r^2 h)$$

When you look at the illustration, you can even see that it looks like one-third.

Hemisphere (c)

Now look at the half-sphere in the tin can. To me it looks like an orange cut in half, sitting in a tuna tin! But you can see, more or less, that the can is a lot more 'full' than it is with the cone. In fact, it's twice as full. The formula for the volume of half a sphere, or a **hemisphere**, is:

$$\frac{2}{3}\pi r^2 h$$

But watch it here – what's h? What is h relative to the sphere? Read the definition above. It's the radius of the sphere! So instead of the volume of a hemisphere being $\frac{2}{3}\pi r^2 h$, we write it as:

$$\frac{2}{3}\pi r^3$$

Sphere (d)

It's an easy jump to go from a hemisphere to a full sphere. It looks a bit odd, but at least you can see how it comes about. The formula for the volume of a sphere is:

$$\frac{4}{3}\pi r^3$$

You can use this list for later reference:

- Circumference of a circle: $2\pi r$
- Area of a circle: πr^2
- Surface area of a cylinder: $(\pi r^2) \times 2 + (2\pi r) \times h$
- Volume of a cylinder: $\pi r^2 h$
- Volume of a cone: $\frac{1}{3}\pi r^2 h$
- Volume of a hemisphere: $\frac{2}{3}\pi r^2 h$, or $\frac{2}{3}\pi r^3$
- Volume of a sphere: $\frac{4}{3}\pi r^2 h$, or $\frac{4}{3}\pi r^3$

EXERCISE 8.10

Find the volume/capacity of the following in m³ or cm³.

(a)   A hemisphere of radius 15cm

(b)   A cone of radius 9cm and height 10cm

(c)   A silo with dimensions as shown

(d)   An industrial gas tank as shown

(e)   A garden hose 50m long and 2cm in diameter

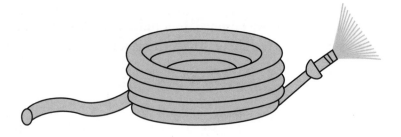

(f)   Convert your answers for (c), (d) and (e) to litres

'Go as far as you can see and when you get there, you'll be able to see further.'

—Zig Ziglar

'When in doubt, run in circles, scream and shout.'

—Laurence J. Peter

'Music is the arithmetic of sounds, as optics is the geometry of light.'

—Claude Debussy

Work, Wages and Taxes

CALCULATING WAGES AND TAXES

Every business, even those that just employ one person, has to calculate the wages each week. This involves correctly calculating the hours worked and applying the appropriate rates of pay for ordinary time and overtime, working out the tax deductions (there are three of them in Ireland) and any other *agreed* deductions that the employer may make, such as savings, insurance premiums or union dues.

Let's begin with calculating gross wages. We'll get to taxes and other deductions later.

Your weekly or monthly wage is calculated by multiplying the hours you have worked, or units you produced, by a suitable rate per hour, or per unit. If you clock in and out each day, a calculation has to be made of the daily hours and these have to be divided into normal and overtime hours (for which you get a premium, usually time and a half or double time).

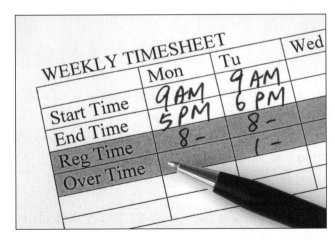

Hourly rate

Adam works 9.00am to 5.00pm daily, with 1 hour for lunch. This means a normal day is 7 hours (i.e. 8 hours less 1 hour for lunch). If Adam works 9 to 5 each day, Monday to Friday, his pay at €10 per hour will be:

$$7 \text{ hours} \times 5 \text{ days} \times €10 \qquad (or \text{ } 35 \text{ normal hours @ } €10)$$
$$\rightarrow €350.00$$

Overtime

If he were to work until 7pm one evening, how much would he be paid?

Overtime like this is usually paid at time and a half. This means that an employee gets an extra half hour's pay for every hour they work. In this example, Adam works 2 hours of overtime on Wednesday, but he will be paid for 2 + (half of 2), or 2 + 1 = 3 hours at €10/hour. This works out at €30 for his extra 2 hours' work.

A simpler way of writing this is:

2 hours	$\times$	1½ premium	$\times$	€10 pay rate	$=$	€30 gross pay

EXERCISE 9.1

Overtime is paid at time and a half. Premium hours are paid at double time. Calculate the gross wages for the following.

(a)   Alan works 34 normal hours and 3 hours of overtime. He is paid €12.50 an hour.

(b)   Brian earns €14.00 an hour for his 35 basic hours. He also worked 7.5 hours of overtime this week.

(c)   Carol's basic week is 40 hours and she also worked for 8 premium hours. Her rate is €15.80 per hour.

(d)   Deirdre works 37.5 hours at €17.50 an hour. She also worked 3 overtime hours and 2 premium hours this week.

Piece rate

Barbara makes skirts in a factory. She is paid €3.50 per skirt made. This is known as a **piece rate**. She is expected to make 100 skirts in a typical week, giving her the same wage as Adam, or €350.00 per 'normal' week, regardless of how long she takes to make the skirts. If she makes 115 skirts in a week, she will be paid:

$$115 \times €3.50 = €402.50$$

Bonus scheme

Some factories operate a bonus scheme, where, for example, Barbara might be paid €3.50 for the first 100 skirts and €4.75 for anything over that. Overtime is not an issue: you're paid per item produced.

A scheme like this is meant to hurry staff along with the basic production so that they produce more skirts in any given week. The business wins, with cheaper basic production, and the employee wins when they work efficiently and quickly. Good for everyone!

How much will Barbara be paid if she makes 115 skirts under this scheme?

$$
\begin{array}{rcl}
100 \times €3.50 & = & €350.00 \\
15 \times €4.75 & = & \underline{€\ \ 71.25} \\
& & \underline{€421.25}
\end{array}
$$

She earns 20% more under the bonus scheme. Which method is better for the business? If Barbara isn't motivated, she won't be energised to work hard under the first scheme, as she gets the same for each skirt she makes. Under the bonus scheme, however, she can see how it will be worthwhile to work that little bit harder, as she only gets the higher rate after making 100 skirts at the lower rates. She gets paid 35% extra for each of the later skirts. It's not as good as time and a half would be (that's 50%), but it's not bad. Win-win!

EXERCISE 9.2

Calculate the wages to be paid.

(a) Amy is paid €4 per item for 120 items and €6 for the extra 25 items she made this week.

(b) Brendan is paid €28.50 per item for the first 15 he makes in a furniture factory plus €40.00 for the extra 6 items this week.

(c) Carlos makes bracelets for €20 each for 25 and €27.50 for 3 extra.

(d) Donna is paid €7.50 for 52 items and €10 for 12 extra.

Commission

If you work in sales, whether it's in a shop or as a representative on the road, you're likely to be paid by **commission**. This is a percentage payment based on your sales for the pay period. This may be paid a week, or more usually a month, in arrears. It is also common for a salesperson to have a low basic pay so that even if business is quiet, they're not left with tiny wages that week or month.

Let's look at an example. Ciaran works for a sweet maker as a salesman, travelling around from shop to shop in a country area. He's paid a basic €500 a month plus 10% commission on all sales he makes. Calculate his total wages for each month if his sales were €15,000 in January and €22,500 in February.

January basic	€ 500	
Commission €15,000 × 10%	€1,500	Total €2,000
February basic	€ 500	
Commission €22,500 × 10%	€2,250	Total €2,750

EXERCISE 9.3

Calculate the gross commission to be paid.

(a) Eric earns 2.5% on €26,300 of carpet sales for the month and a basic of €250.

(b) Frances works for an estate agent and earns 15% on €32,300 plus her monthly basic of €400.

(c) Geraldine earns 25% on boutique sales of €2,675 this week, with no basic.

(d) Harriet is the shop manager and has no basic but gets 3.5% commission on all sales of €56,500 this month.

> ## GROSS PAY

The above methods of calculating pay all make up the employee's gross pay. The **gross pay** is the amount used as the starting point for calculating the various taxes due. But what is gross pay? What's in there? We've seen that it includes per hour and piece rate wages and commissions. I use a mnemonic to remember the eight items on the following list, which contains most of what you'll come across in any typical wages office:

> ## BBC B(reakfast) SHOW
>
> | | |
> |---|---|
> | B-ack pay | S-alary |
> | B-onus | H-oliday pay |
> | C-ommission | O-vertime |
> | B-enefit in kind | W-ages |

Back pay is arrears due for some reason, now being paid. This could be a raise negotiated by the union, to take effect from 1 March. If today is April or May, there will be an element of back pay to be made up.

Benefit in kind is different: it's not a cash payment at all, but a benefit, or value, given in kind (i.e. in goods) or in some other way. For example, workers in a butcher shop might get free meat every week, bank workers get cheaper loans and airline workers get cheap or even free flights. The most common one, though, is the company car. The Revenue has a formula for calculating a pay equivalent for the use of the car. It's based on a percentage of the open market value of the car, when new, and it decreases on a sliding scale depending on how many business miles – oops, kilometres – you drive. Business kilometres are allowed, but you're being taxed on the use of the car for private or personal purposes.

> **Revenue** is the name given to the operating arm of the Revenue Commissioners, who are responsible for assessing and collecting all taxes in Ireland.

For example, a sales rep driving up to 32,000km a year is taxed on 24% of the original new value of the car. If the car cost €25,000, then the annual income addition is:

$$€25,000 \times 24\% = €6,000 \, a \, year$$

Now before you gasp at the savagery of that, remember that it's €6,000 taxed at most, at 41%, or €2,460, a year. That's equivalent to having a car for just €47 a week. Not so savage after all, is it? As the distances driven increase to 40,000, and 48,000 or above, then the 24% rate reduces to 18% and 12% and finally as low as 6% for long-distance drivers. That's just €12 a week.

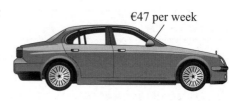

€47 per week

PAYROLL TAXES

There are three payroll taxes in Ireland today:

- **Income tax**, known as Pay As You Earn (PAYE)
- **Pay Related Social Insurance** (PRSI)
- **Universal Social Charge** (USC), the newest tax, introduced in 2011

Statutory deductions

The above three taxes are called **statutory deductions**. This means they are deducted by law – every employer *must* deduct them every time he or she pays you.

Non-statutory deductions

Non-statutory deductions are voluntary deductions from your wages that can be made by your employer, but only with your written permission. They include such things as … well, let's try another odd little mnemonic.

CV ReSULTS

Again, you'll find this list covers most of the common deductions:

C-redit union or similar payment

V-HI or other health insurance

Re-payment of company loans

S-ocial club dues

U-nion dues

L-ife assurance premiums

T-ea money/canteen

S-avings

INCOME TAX (PAYE)

Often referred to as PAYE, this is the main payroll tax. All earned income is subject to income tax at twin rates, which for several years have been 20% and 41%. The Minister for Finance may well change these in the Budget, so let's just use these rates for the examples and exercises. The format of the calculations will remain the same even if the rates change year to year.

However, I'll use a fictional standard rate cut-off point (SRCOP) for simplicity's sake. That point is €32,000 for a single person. Married couples and civil partners may transfer up to €9,000 from one partner to the other, giving a maximum SRCOP of €41,000 for any one individual.

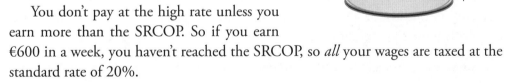

- The standard rate is 20% and, for single individuals, applies to €32,000 of income per year. This threshold is applied in weekly or monthly 'slices' by dividing the total by 52 for the weekly 'slice' (€615.38 per week) or by 12 for the monthly 'slice' (€2,666.66 per month). This sum is called the standard rate cut-off point, or SRCOP.

- The higher rate is currently 41% and this applies to all income over the SRCOP.

You don't pay at the high rate unless you earn more than the SRCOP. So if you earn €600 in a week, you haven't reached the SRCOP, so *all* your wages are taxed at the standard rate of 20%.

Wages	€600.00
Tax @ 20%	€120.00

This is called your **gross tax**. Gross means big, because it has to be reduced by your tax credits (see below).

If you get a bonus next week of €100, making your total wages €700, then you pay tax like this:

Wages as normal	€600.00
Add bonus this week	100.00
Total gross pay	€700.00

Tax on SRCOP	(32,000 ÷ 52)	615.38	@ 20% =	€123.08
Tax on excess		84.62	@ 41% =	34.69
Total gross pay		€700.00		
Gross tax				€157.77

This gross tax is then reduced by a discount, called your **tax credit**. Tax credits are given depending on your status (see below).

TAX CREDITS

The following is taken from the Revenue table of tax credits for 2012.

Single person	€1,650
Married person or civil partner	€3,300
PAYE tax credit	€1,650
Age tax credit if single	€ 245
Age tax credit if married	€ 490

The typical single person with a job just gets the personal credit of €1,650 (just for having a pulse) and the PAYE credit, also €1,650 (for having a job). It's a total of €3,300 per year, or €63.46 per week (divide by 52).

These rates are applied on a weekly or monthly basis (divide by 12) and occasionally, but rarely, fortnightly (divide by 26). I say rarely, but many of the employees of the Health Services Executive, one of the largest employers in the country, are paid fortnightly.

Anyway, the annual SRCOP is also divided into weekly/monthly/fortnightly slices in this way and applied week by week/month by month, etc. on a **cumulative** basis. This means that each week, the tax is calculated based on *all* money earned since 1 January each year. This cumulative system ensures that a constant, self-correcting mechanism operates. While most businesses today will use a payroll software program, it's also possible for small businesses to calculate this by hand, using a form known as a **Tax Deduction Card**. Copies can be downloaded from www.revenue.ie/en/tax/it/leaflets/. Some of these can be completed and saved on your computer, while others can be printed to be completed by hand.

A page from the official Revenue Tax Deduction Card is shown on page 156 of the appendix for illustration purposes. As you can see, it's extremely cramped for handwritten figures, so I've laid it out more simply in a spreadsheet just for PAYE and PRSI calculation in the appendix (see page 157). I've included a simple sample for learning on, with a cut-off of €600 a week and credits of €60. There's also a normal one with a proper cut-off and credits. Finally, I've included a blank sample so you or your teacher can photocopy and use it for your own class exercises. The columns are exactly the same as the normal Revenue Card.

CALCULATING PAY AS YOU EARN (PAYE)

You can calculate PAYE using the Tax Deduction Card. At first glance it may seem complicated, but once you get the idea it really is very simple. Remember, it's been used for years by every corner shop owner up and down the country, so it has to be easy.

- Enter the gross wage in column G (gross pay this period).
- Add this to the figure in last week's column H, giving the new cumulative gross pay to date. (The next six columns are also cumulative.)
- Compare this figure to the standard rate cut-off point in column I. Tax the *lower* of the two at 20%, the standard rate. Put your answer in column J.
- If column H is bigger than column I, tax the excess at the higher rate of 41% and put this figure in column K. Otherwise, leave K blank.
- Add columns J and K together: J + K = column L, the gross tax.
- Deduct the cumulative tax credit, pre-printed, to leave cumulative tax in column N.
- Deduct last week's figure, in the *same* column, which leaves tax deducted this period (column O). Or if last week's figure in column N was bigger, insert the minus answer into column P as tax refunded this period.

Once you practise this a little, it becomes an easy and dependable way to calculate the weekly tax deduction. Follow the worked samples on pages 159 and 161.

Points to Remember

- Always use a sharp pencil, as errors are easier to correct.
- If you've just written down a number, use it (the only exception is calculating the high rate of tax).
- Always check your final tax figure against this week's gross wage. If it looks wrong, it probably is – but maybe it's not, so check it.
- When practising, do one entire week at a time. In the real world, that's how things are. Do one week at a time.
- A Tax Deduction Card can get cramped and untidy very easily, so make your writing small and neat – this isn't an essay!

PAY RELATED SOCIAL INSURANCE (PRSI)

Another payroll tax, PRSI is designed to insure workers against being unemployed and pay him/her a pay-related dole amount, depending on their level of pay. Alas, the 'pay-related' element didn't last too long. With the recent introduction of the Universal Social Charge, PRSI rates have fallen sharply. The employer, however, still contributes 10.75% on all earnings, making PRSI unique in that it taxes two people, employer and employee, based on the same income.

How to calculate PRSI

Each year, the Revenue publishes a table of rates for PRSI to reflect any changes made in the government's annual budget. An extract from the table of PRSI contribution rates for 2013 is shown below.

Private and Some Public Sector Employments					
Non-cumulative Weekly Earnings Band	PRSI Subclasses	How Much of Weekly Earnings	Employee %	Employer %	Employee & Employer %
Up to €37.99	J0	ALL	0	0.50	0.50
€38 – €352	A0	ALL	0	4.25	4.25
€352.01 – €356	AX	ALL	4.00	4.25	8.25
€356.01 – €500	AL	ALL	4.00	10.75	14.75
More than €500	A1	ALL	4.00	10.75	14.75

Source: www.welfare.ie
Note: Class AX applies to a range of just €4.

If you earn €400 per week, you pay as follows:

Charge employee at class AL   €400 × 4%   = €16.00

Charge employer at 10.75%   €400 × 10.75% = €43.00

If you earn €575.00 you pay at class A1, which happens to be the same in percentage terms:

Charge employee at class A1   €575 × 4%   = €23.00

Charge employer at 10.75%   €575 × 10.75% = €61.81

The recording of the different classes each week is important because they affect your entitlements later – perhaps many years later, even as late as pension age. Pay attention and get it right. Your employees depend on it.

UNIVERSAL SOCIAL CHARGE (USC)

This new payroll tax was introduced in 2011 and is a broader tax, with fewer exemptions than either PRSI or PAYE. It applies on a sliding scale.

Tax Year 2011/2012	Rate of USC
Income up to €10,036.00 (€193 per week)	2%
On next €5,980 (€115.00 per week)	4%
Income above €16,016.00 (€308.00 per week)	7%

The Universal Social Charge has a separate card all of its own. This has a bit more space and is more practical than the PAYE tax deduction card (see page 163 in the appendix).

Calculating USC

The first thing to remember with USC is that it's cumulative. Each employee's card will have the 2%, 4% and 7% thresholds indicated on it and it may not be the standard amounts, so check the documentation carefully for each employee.

The second thing to remember is that this is a bit awkward and therefore shouldn't be rushed. Work your way through my explanation following the figures on the sample card (see page 164). Use your calculator as you go to help you see what's happening. Please don't blame me: it's a Revenue form!

1. If we follow the example shown (from www.welfare.ie), enter the gross pay (€250) in the first column (Gross Pay) and add to last week's total in the second column (Cumulative Gross Pay for USC to Date), except of course in week 1. Note that this gross pay may not be the same as for PAYE, so again, be careful.

2. The next column (in red), Cumulative USC COP 1 (2%), records the weekly accumulating first threshold. The normal is €193 per week. If this is less than

the gross pay, calculate €193 at 2% and enter €3.96 in the next column. (Incidentally, COP stands for cut-off point.)

3. The next section (in blue) starts with the Cumulative 4% COP at €308 per week. In the example shown, the gross pay is only €250, so it doesn't reach the threshold of €308. Just tax the excess over the lower €193 amount: €250 − €193 = €57 and €57 @ 4% = €2.28 as shown, marked with an asterisk (*). As we've now taxed the full gross pay, add the USC amounts together and enter the total into Cumulative USC (black). As this is week 1, €6.14 is 'USC deducted this period'.

4. This procedure is repeated in week 2 of the example. Skip to week 3 and enter gross pay of €475. Cumulative is now €975. The 2% threshold is 3 × €193, or €579, which gives us €11.58. The 4% threshold has reached €924. But we've already taxed €574, so deduct this and calculate 4% on the remainder (this *is* awkward!), which we tax to give €13.80, like this:

$$€924 − €579 = €345$$

$$€345 @ 4\% = €13.80$$

5. Finally, we have to tax the remainder of the €975 gross at 7%:

$$€975 − €924 = €51 \quad \text{and} \quad €51 @ 7\% = €3.57$$

6. Now just add the three USC amounts together:

$$€11.58 + €13.80 + €3.57 = €28.95$$

7. That's the total USC due since 1 January. But we have already paid €12.28 up to last week, so deduct last week from this week to give you 'USC deducted (or refunded) this week':

$$€28.95 − €12.28 = €16.67$$

Work through the weeks to be sure you know what's going on here. I found that repeating it several times is the only way to get your head around it. In many ways this is where you see the value of computer payroll software. It handles this for you and gets it right every time. However, it's always good to understand what the computer is doing 'under the bonnet'.

So there you have the three taxes: income tax/PAYE, PRSI and USC. If you're a single person earning a modest €500 a week, this is what your payslip would look like:

Gross pay		500.00
Deductions:		
€500 taxed at 20% (all within the SRCOP)		100.00
Less tax credits $\left(\dfrac{€3,300}{52}\right)$		63.46
Net income tax		36.54
PRSI @ 4%		20.00
USC €193 × 2% =	3.86	
€115 × 4% =	4.60	
€500 − €308 = €192 × 7% =	13.44 21.90	
Total deductions		78.44
Net (or take-home) pay		€421.56

Just for the record, this represents taxes of over 15.7% of gross pay. Ouch!

Notice the payslip. It's a legal requirement that every payment to an employee comes with a written payslip showing how the net amount is arrived at. It should include:

- Gross pay, usually split into its elements (e.g. basic + overtime)
- PAYE deducted
- PRSI deducted
- USC deducted
- Any other non-tax deductions (or additions like expenses)
- Net amount paid, called net pay or take-home pay

It should be clear and neat and easy to read!

EXERCISE 9.4

Using the information given below for Peter O'Connor, calculate his gross pay, PAYE, PRSI and USC. In addition, do full payslips, leading to net pay, for weeks 1, 2, 3 and 4. You will also need to work out his tax credits using the list on page 98.

Week 1: Peter's normal (5-day) weekly pay is €550. He pays €5 a week to the company social club and €18 in health insurance. He has no extras or deductions this week. He is single with a SRCOP of €32,000.

Week 2: Same as week 1, but with the addition of a new year bonus of €185, which is taxable.

Week 3: Peter misses 2 days due to illness – he only gets paid when he works.

Week 4: Peter's December sales generated commission of €328.00, to be paid this week with his full week's pay.

'If I'm paying twice as much tax as you, it's probably because I'm earning twice as much.'

—Robert Jordan

'I'm thankful for the taxes I pay because it means that I'm employed.'

—Nancy Carmody

'Rich bachelors should be heavily taxed. It's not fair that some men should be happier than others!'

—Oscar Wilde

Value Added Tax (VAT)

CHAPTER 10

Before starting this chapter, it's a good idea to revise Chapter 7 on percentages. Everything about VAT is done in percentages. In business, if you don't understand percentages and how to manipulate them, you're lost. Percentages affect everything you do:

- Setting prices
- Deciding your mark-up
- Charging and reclaiming VAT
- Discounts given and received
- Deducting PAYE, PRSI and Universal Social Charge
- Measuring profit
- Measuring growth
- Controlling costs

VAT

Let's begin with how **Value Added Tax (VAT)** works, because most business transactions will have VAT added and that VAT will show up on the invoices. Have a look at the following diagram – we'll use it to explain how this tax operates and, most importantly, who pays it.

VAT SYSTEM

		Farmer	Sawmill	Wholesaler	Shop
Sell for		100	200	400	800
Plus VAT	A	23	46	92	184
		123	246	492	984
Buy/cost		0	100	200	400
Plus VAT	B	0	23	46	92
		0	123	246	492
Expenses:					
Power (VAT @ 13.5%)				74	
Packaging (VAT @ 23%)					104
Plus VAT	C			10	24
				84	124
Pay to Revenue	A−B−C	23	23	36	68
		23 − 0 = 23	46 − 23 = 23	92 − 46 − 10 = 36	184 − 92 − 24 = 68

1. We begin by assuming a farmer cuts down a tree on his land and sells it for €100 to a local sawmill. He charges VAT at the standard rate of 23% (€23), making a total of €123. The farmer pays the €23 to Revenue (the taxman to you and me!). He has no other expenses. (An absurdly unreal assumption, I know, but humour me just for this example.)

2. The sawmill cuts the tree into planks and sells them to a wholesaler for €200, again plus 23%, or €46. The mill owner deducts the €23 he paid the farmer and pays the remainder, €23 (€46 − €23), to the Revenue.

3. The wholesaler sells the planks to a shop, your local builders' provider, for €400 plus 23%, making a total of €492. The wholesaler has also paid his electricity bill of €74 plus 13.5% (total €84). Before the wholesaler pays the tax, he will deduct the VAT he paid to *both* the sawmill and the electricity company:

VAT on sale		€ 92
VAT on purchase	−46	
VAT on electricity	−10	56
Net VAT due to Revenue		€ 36

4. Next, the shop sells the planks to you and me for the outrageous total of €984: that's €800 plus 23%, or €184. It's worth noting that the VAT rate never changes, as the rate is determined by the nature of the goods being sold and we are selling and reselling the same tree/timber right through this example. The shop has also just bought some packing materials and paid €104 plus 23%, or €24. So their cheque to the Revenue will be:

VAT on sale		€184
VAT on purchase	−92	
VAT on packaging	−24	116
Net VAT due to Revenue		€ 68

To summarise the above, total sales, total VAT charged and total VAT deducted are shown below, along with the total VAT paid to the Revenue.

	Sales	VAT Added	VAT Claimed	Revenue Cheque
Farmer	100	23	nil	23
Sawmill	200	46	(23)	23
Wholesaler	400	92	(56)	36
Shop	800	184	(116)	68
You and me	Not registered for VAT, so no reclaim!			
Totals	1,500	345	(195)	150
Add paid to Revenue: by electricity co.				10
by packaging co.				24
Total VAT paid to Revenue				€184

You'll notice that this is the exact amount added by the shop and charged to you and I, the ultimate consumers/users of the product. We pay *all* the VAT that was paid to the Revenue by each of the businesses in the supply chain in turn. Sickening, isn't it? Well, yes, but that's what a spending tax is supposed to do: charge those who use the product. VAT is a means of collecting the tax. It's applied as the product proceeds through the cycle of manufacture and distribution. Each trader/business adds value, if only by making the product available at your local store, and pays the tax on their part of the added value.

DEFINITIONS

When we talk about VAT, we refer to net price, VAT-inclusive price, VAT-exclusive price and so on. It can be confusing, so get to grips with it as early as you can. Doing the exercises will help too.

Sticking with our timber example, the farmer charges the sawmill €100 for the tree and then he adds VAT of 23%.

€100 is the **VAT-exclusive (or net) price**

€23 is the **VAT**

€123 is the **VAT-inclusive (or gross) price**

It's absolutely essential for you to realise that the 23% calculation only works in *one* direction. If you're told that the over-the-counter price of an item is €12.30 after VAT at 23%, then it's easy to recognise that that represents €10.00 for the goods plus €2.30 VAT, making the total €12.30.

But to calculate the VAT included in that price, you can't just get 23% of €12.30. That's not how it works. Look: 23% of €12.30 is €2.83, not €2.30! Get out your calculator: check it.

Remember The Model from Chapter 7 on percentages (pages 63–4)? Let's see how this example fits:

The Model

Net sales	100	A
VAT @ 23%	23	B
Total sales price	123	C

Obviously, here the €12.30 fits as C.

So 12.30 ÷ 123 × 100 = 10.00

This means the VAT-exclusive price is €10.00. Now do this exercise on your own.

EXERCISE 10.1

Calculate the VAT on the following sale ticket prices (VAT inclusive), assuming three rates for each example: 23%, 13.5% and 8%.

(a)   €3.00

(b)   €7.00

(c)   €12.00

(d)   €23.00

(e)   €17.50

(f)   €28.95

(g)   €78.65

(h)   €65.53

(i)   €126.80

(j)   €256.44

(k)   €399.00

(l)   €1,234.56

'VAT = Vulture Added Tax.'

—Steve Fowler

'When it comes to age, I say I'm 49 plus VAT.'

—Lionel Blair

Interesting Interest, Insurance and Depreciation

Money makes money, and when it does, the money it makes is called **interest**.

When you put money in a bank for a time, they pay you interest. When you borrow money from a bank, you pay them interest. Needless to say, you pay them more than they pay you, but that's how banks make money. The difference is their **margin**.

Our task here is to understand interest and know how to calculate it. Interest calculations comprise three elements:

- The money itself, called the **principal**
- The **percentage rate** charged or earned
- The **period**, or time, during which you or the bank has the money

SIMPLE INTEREST

The easiest to calculate is **simple interest**. This is where you earn interest and it's paid to you at the end of the period. In this case, the amount in your account remains the same. The bank may also add the money to your account, but you still only earn interest on the original deposit.

Let's do an example and then explain what's going on.

I leave €1,000 on deposit in the bank for 1 year @ 10% interest. The interest rate is usually understood to be for a year, or 'per annum' (Latin meaning 'for a year'). It's often shown as p.a. The formula is simple:

$$P \text{ (principal)} \times R \text{ (rate)} \times T \text{ (time in years)}$$

It's usually written as:

$$\frac{P \times R \times T}{100}$$

Or even more simply:

$$\frac{PRT}{100}$$

If the interest rate is written in decimal form, we can simplify the formula still further to just PRT, as follows:

$$
\begin{array}{ccccccc}
P & & R & & T & & \\
\text{€1,000} & \times & 0.1 & \times & 1 & = & \text{€100}
\end{array}
$$

In this case, I earned €100 interest for the year. (By the way, if you can find any bank willing to pay 10% per annum, please give me a call!)

If I leave my money in the bank for 2 years, my interest calculation is:

$$
\begin{array}{ccccc}
\text{principal} & \times & \text{rate} & \times & \text{time} \\
\text{€1,000} & \times & 10\% & \times & 2
\end{array}
$$

This simple formula of principal by rate by time allows us to easily calculate what the interest will be for any period, long or short. In the real world, money is rarely left in the bank for an even year or an exact number of whole years. The period will almost always be irregular. But if we use the simple interest formula, we can easily work out the interest due.

Let's say I leave my €1,000 in the bank for 9 months. We adjust the previous figures as follows:

$$
\begin{array}{ccccc}
\text{principal} & \times & \text{rate} & \times & \text{time} \\
\text{€1,000} & \times & 10\% & \times & \frac{9}{12} \text{ (nine-twelfths of a year)}
\end{array}
$$

The period here is expressed as a fraction of a full year because the rate is a rate per year. Again, in the real world banks actually calculate interest on a daily basis. In this case the fraction would be $\frac{273}{365}$ (calculate the number of days in 9 months). The advantage of this is that you can take your money out at any time and the bank can calculate precisely how much interest you've earned. With their computers, they can even take account of multiple lodgements and withdrawals, allowing for daily amounts added to and taken from your account, all earning interest for the number of days that the money spends in your account.

EXERCISE 11.1

Calculate the simple interest correct to two decimal places (i.e. euros and cents).

(a) €13,000 for 1 year at 7.5% p.a.

(b) €4,500 for 3 years at 8% p.a.

(c) €950 for 5 years at 11.5% p.a.

(d) €5,600 for 6 months at 12.5% p.a.

(e) €36,500 for 2 years and 8 months at 9.5% p.a.

Interest rate changes are regularly reported in the news because interest is an important factor in many family budgets. The two main rates we hear about are the cheapest one, mortgage interest, and the dearest one, credit card interest.

Mortgage interest is important because although the annual rate is generally quite small (currently as low as 5% or 6%), it applies to a large principal – most of the cost of the family home – so you could be paying mortgage interest on €200,000 or more. Even at very low interest rates, that's a lot of money out of your monthly income.

Credit card interest is entirely different because it tends to have a smaller principal, as it's made up of mostly small amounts of daily spending. However, the rates charged can be enormous – one hears of rates as high as 23%. In this case, the interest on even a modest unpaid balance can be huge, so be careful of credit card debt.

COMPOUND INTEREST

Relatively few banks use simple interest. Instead, they offer interest on the principal but leave that interest in the account. So for the next period, the principal has grown by the interest credited last time. This is called **compound interest**, as it gets added to your balance every period for which it is calculated.

Let's look again at the simple interest example: €1,000 for 1 year @ 10%. But now we're calculating both the interest and the revised principal or balance:

$$€1,000 × 0.1 × 1 = €100 \text{ interest}$$

But we're adding the original principal of €1,000 = €1,100.

This revises the formula to:

$$P + (PRT)$$

That seems straightforward, but (there's always a but!) look what happens when we try to calculate the figures for, say, 3 years:

Year 1

Principal 1	€1,000
Add interest (P1 × R × T)	100
Principal for year 2	1,100

Year 2

Add interest (P2 × R × T)	110
Principal for year 3	1,210

Year 3

Add interest (P3 × R × T)	121
Final amount end year 3	€1,331

So you see, you earn interest in increasing amounts because each year, you earn interest on last year's interest as well as your original principal. As I said at the start of the chapter, money makes money.

To give you an idea of what this would look like on a statement from your bank, let's present it as a bank might. Lodged amounts are those added to your bank balance, so in this example all amounts will be 'lodged'.

Date	Details	Lodged	Withdrawn	Balance
Day 1	Initial lodgement	1,000		1,000
Year 1	Interest for year	100		1,100
Year 2	Interest for year	110		1,210
Year 3	Interest for year	121		1,331

Each year-end balance is the principal for the following year's interest calculation.

EXERCISE 11.2

What would the example above look like if it was calculated on simple interest? Remember, in simple interest the opening principal is used *each* year.

A shorter, easier and quicker way to calculate compound interest

The example above is the long form of the compound interest calculation and you'll agree that it's a bit cumbersome. There's a shorter way and you'll need a calculator for this.

Using the letters as shown above, the final amount will be:

$$P\left(1 + \frac{R}{100}\right)^{T}$$

This is usually written with an n (for number of years) replacing the letter T and the final amount is represented by the letter A. So it becomes:

$$A = P\left(1 + \frac{R}{100}\right)^{n}$$

Take our easy example from above: €1,000 @ 10% for 3 years, which gave us €1,331. Now let's calculate it using the formula:

$$A = P\left(1 + \frac{R}{100}\right)^{n}$$

$$= 1,000\left(1 + \frac{10}{100}\right)^{3}$$

$$= 1,000(1 + 0.1)^{3}$$

$$= 1,000(1.1)^{3}$$

$$= 1,000 \times 1.331$$

$$= 1,331$$

Using your calculator (if you have a scientific one), you can use the power function to enter 1.1^{3}. Otherwise use the constant function, as explained in Chapter 2:

$$1.1 \times \times 1,000 = = = \text{(one equals sign for each year)}$$

$$\text{Answer: } 1,331, \text{ meaning } €1,331$$

EXERCISE 11.3

Calculate the compound interest and the final amount in euros and cents.

(a) €4,000 for 3 years at 15% p.a.

(b) €6,300 for 4 years at 8% p.a.

(c) €3,750 for 5 years at 13.5% p.a.

(d) €17,875 for 2 ½ years at 9%

(e)   A client earns a total of €3,310.00 after 3 years at 10%. How much did she invest?

> ## INSURANCE

Imagine a small community. They all have the usual health problems, some minor and some more serious. If everyone pays into a scheme they'll build up a fund so that when one person or family has a serious need, like a hospital operation, they can claim off the scheme to pay the bills. They just continue to pay their contribution into the scheme every month. That's insurance at work: when lots of people contribute into a fund that can be called on when you have a problem, whether it's a car crash, flood damage or hospital surgery.

Insurance companies are just big fund managers for their customers. They charge a premium for the cover and they take a charge out of the fund each year to pay their salaries and expenses. The premium they charge is based, more or less, on the value of the thing they are insuring.

Types of insurance

- There is insurance for many risks encountered in business. We're all familiar with **motor insurance**, which covers us – or more importantly, the other guy, the third party – when we have an accident (see below).
- There's also **home insurance, health insurance** and **life insurance**.
- **Permanent health insurance** (sometimes called **income protection**) covers you if you can't work because of serious ill health or injury.
- **Mortgage protection insurance** is a form of life insurance, which clears your mortgage if you should die.
- In business, if you have any employees you must have **employer's liability insurance**, which covers your workers against injury while at work.
- **Burglary** (guess!).
- **Public liability** in case any customer or member of the public injures themselves on your property (slips in the toilet, falls on the stairs or chokes on your speciality sandwich).
- **Fire and engineering insurance** covers you if you have a fire or if any machinery causes damage, say from an explosion or a part breaking off and injuring someone.
- **Cash insurance** against theft.
- **Loss of profits insurance** against having to close after, say, a storm or floods.

Third party

Why do we say 'third' party? Think about the contract – it's made between:

1. The insurance company, the *first* party (party is just a fancy legal word for person)
2. You, the *second* party
3. And then, when you injure somebody or damage their property, they become the *third* party

Say your house has a rebuild cost of €200,000. Home insurance will be charged at a tiny rate, perhaps as little as 0.2%. Calculate the annual premium.

$$€200,000 \times 0.2\% = €400$$

In the real world, insurance tends to be quoted at a rate per thousand rather than per cent, like we might be used to. So in the above example the rate would be $\frac{€2}{€1,000}$. The premium is calculated by reference to what it will cost to replace the lost item. Thus, a house isn't insured for its market value, which, as we saw during the Celtic Tiger years, could be huge. Rather, it's calculated on the replacement value – the rebuild cost – which might be as little as half or less of the market value. A building is a building regardless of the address (which can inflate values). But houses can be of a different quality and may cost more or less than usual to rebuild, so the rates can vary. For example, a timber house will cost less to rebuild than a brick house.

Insurance companies apply a basic rate for their services. They also charge more for bigger risks. If your life insurance (which takes account of age, gender, health history and whether or not you smoke) normally costs, say, €1,000 a year but you tell the company that you're into free-style rock climbing in the Alps, then they'll **load** your premium because you live a risky life! They may even refuse to cover you at all. Or let's say you're a scuba diver: they may add a loading of 5% or 10%. Or they may exclude death while diving from the cover. Other than that, the premium will remain the same. Business is business!

Finally, the government applies a **surcharge** or **levy** on all insurances. This is to provide a fund to cover, for example, those injured by uninsured drivers. It's illegal to drive a car without at least having third party cover. Nobody cares if you lose your car or if you get injured, but you must insure the person on the footpath injured by your car. If you don't, the fund does. The levy can be about 2% of the original premium.

EXERCISE 11.4

Calculate the premiums for each of the following.

(a) John's house is valued at €150,000. Fire premium of €11.80 per thousand. Levy 2%.

(b) Louise's jewellery and art, worth €20,000, covered against robbery for €1.50 per thousand. Levy 2%.

(c) Frank's golf clubs and gear, worth €2,000. Premium €1.50 per thousand. Levy 1.5%.

(d) Jack is 20 and driving his first car. Basic insurance (third party only) is costing €600 with a 40% loading because he's under 25 and a 3% loading on top because he lives in Dublin. However, he got a new customer discount of 5% of the total premium. The 2% levy applies.

(e) Jack wants comprehensive cover next year. The car will be worth €8,000 and cover will cost an extra €7.20 per thousand. He will lose his discount, but he will qualify for a no claims bonus of 12.5%. The levy will apply, but at 2.5%.

DEPRECIATION

In accounting, something you own is called an **asset**. If you buy a car, you pay the money on day 1. At the end of the first year, any car owner or garage salesman will tell you the car is only worth about 80% of what you paid. In other words, you have suffered **depreciation** of 20% of the cost (though 'suffered' is a bit harsh – after all, you've driven the car for perhaps 20,000 miles).

We calculate depreciation for two reasons:

- To reflect the value of the car at the end of the year
- To reflect the cost for the year of using this valuable asset

Depreciation is applied on virtually all assets. Land doesn't lose value, but pretty much everything else does. Property sometimes *gains* value, as values generally rise over time. (The recent property crash is the first time in Ireland that values have actually fallen.)

There are two common methods of calculating depreciation:

- **Straight line method**, where we simply divide the cost by the expected useful life of the asset and take that amount each year until the value is nil. This suits a computer program, which you buy for 2 or 3 years and consume 1 year's worth each year. Simple.

- **Reducing balance method** (always used for cars), where we take a fixed percentage of each year's reducing value until we sell the old car for whatever we can get. This is usually done by trade-in: when we buy a new(er) car, the garage buys the old one from us.

Whichever method we use, we should use the same method for the entire life of the asset so that our business results will be consistent.

Look at the example to see the difference between the two methods.

Straight line @ 20% €		Reducing balance @ 20% €
20,000	Cost	20,000
4,000	Depreciation year 1	4,000
16,000	Net book value year 1	16,000
4,000	Depreciation year 2	3,200
12,000	Net book value year 2	12,800
4,000	Depreciation year 3	2,560
8,000	Net book value year 3	10,240
4,000	Depreciation year 4	2,048
4,000	Net book value year 4	8,192
4,000	Depreciation year 5	1,638
Nil	Net book value year 5	€6,554

As you can see from this example, the two methods give very different answers. When you think about it, some assets have a reasonable resale value even after several years of use. A car is a good example: it retains some value, even as parts or scrap. However, think about a 5-year-old laptop computer. No thank you! You can't give it away: old software, old technology, old screen, old memory, etc. In addition, some things expire after some years. A software licence is one example, or a property leased for 10 years. In year 11, you're out. You no longer have rights.

However, some businesses make the two show a residual value, as happens naturally with reducing balance calculations. **Residual value** is what's left at the end of an asset's useful life. You deduct an estimate of that value before applying depreciation using the straight line approach.

Let's calculate straight line depreciation on a machine costing €19,000 with an estimated residual value of €3,000 after 4 years.

Cost	19,000		
Less estimated residual value	3,000		
Effective depreciable value	16,000		
Depreciation year 1 (1 quarter)	4,000		
Net book value year 1	12,000	+	3,000
Depreciation year 2 (1 quarter)	4,000		
Net book value year 2	8,000	+	3,000
Depreciation year 3 (1 quarter)	4,000		
Net book value year 3	4,000	+	3,000
Depreciation year 4 (1 quarter)	4,000		
Net book value year 4	Nil	+	3,000

Always remember that we have deducted €3,000, so the book value in each case is €3,000 more than shown. The depreciation is more accurate, as it takes account of the expected trade-in value remaining after 4 years of use.

EXERCISE 11.5

Calculate the depreciation and the net book value for each year for each of the following assets using *both* methods (straight line and reducing balance). For each asset, state which one you think is the more appropriate method.

(a) Car costing €12,000, expected life (normal for cars) 5 years, at 20%

(b) A mahogany boardroom table, 10 years, cost €5,000, residual value €1,000

(c) Computer for advanced graphics costing €8,500, life 4 years, residual value €500

(d) 4-year licence for software for the graphics computer, costing €5,800, residual value nil

(e) Sandpit costing €120,000 expected to give out in 5 years, residual value €25,000

'Fun is like life insurance – the older you get, the more it costs.'

— Kin Hubbard

Budgets for Home and Business

All the best businesses do budgets, governments do budgets and schools do budgets, so, why not you and me?

The idea is simple:

- We write down our weekly, monthly or yearly income (from *all* sources).
- Then we write down our expected, or planned, expenses.
- Take one from the other and see what's left. Add in your bank balance.
- Done!

Sounds simple, doesn't it? Well, it is … and it isn't.

Income is usually easy. Dad's take-home pay, plus Mam's take-home pay, plus any government payouts, like Child Benefit, and any odd bits from other sources. What other sources? Well, how about hobbies like selling a painting on eBay, giving a few guitar lessons or selling some organic vegetables from your eco-garden; or what about interest on savings, dividends on shares, winnings on the horses or even the odd gift or inheritance? Remember, this is *your* budget. It's not for any official purpose, so put everything down there – *all* your income.

Let's look at an example.

Budget for John and Alice Smith for 3 months ended 31 March				
INCOME	**Jan**	**Feb**	**Mar**	**Total (1)**
Salaries (2)				
John (3)	3,240	3,240	3,550	10,030
Alice (4)	1,120	1,620	1,120	3,860
Bank interest	–	–	60	60
Other (art classes)	100	100	100	300
Total income (5)	4,460	4,960	4,830	14,250

Notes:

(1) Always include a total column. Apart from anything else, it helps you prove your figures because everything has to tot down and across to €14,250. It also helps to summarise the data nicely: 'Wow, I'll take home over €10,000 in just 3 months!' Feels good!

(2) Show separately for every earner in the house.

(3) John expects a raise in March, so put that in there.

(4) Alice is due her bonus in February. Put that in too.

(5) Pay attention to layout generally. Use precise headings, including a description of the document (Budget), the client's name (John and Alice) and the dates/period covered. Then use columns for each month, a total column, single lines around the totals and clear, brief narrations (see the full worked example on page 129).

You can see here how it works for income. You put in what you *expect* will happen for each month. Everything is a forecast and may or may not happen as you expect, so be a bit conservative (less enthusiastic) when forecasting income. Also, do your figures in round euros – never show cents in a budget. Remember, it's a budget – a forecast (a guess, albeit an intelligent guess!). It may even be adequate to show all figures to the nearest €10, so everything ends in a zero. It's much easier to work with, and when talking about €14,000, what's a tenner one way or the other? Notice that in the example there's nothing more precise than €10 and no cents to be seen. And never put two zeros after every figure (e.g. €10.00). If you're eliminating cents, just leave out the decimal point and the zeros altogether. (For bigger business budgets you might have no figures under €100 or even €1,000. In this case, €10,000 would appear as €10 in a column headed €'000, indicating all figures are in thousands.)

EXERCISE 12.1

Give all figures in euros (no cents).

(a)   Prepare an income budget for the Connolly family for April, May and June. Alan works from home as a small-time organic gardener with irregular income. He expects to earn €1,200 in April and May and €3,000 in June. He also earns €300 a month as a musician. Mary is a marketing executive and takes home €3,500 a month. She expects a tax-free bonus of €2,000 in May.

(b)   Donal and Elisa Flanagan have one child and receive Child Benefit from the state of €240 a month. Donal takes home €2,200 a month and Elisa €1,750. Donal expects a 10% pay cut in August. Prepare the income budget for July to September.

(c)   Geraldine and Harry Ingles are partners in a beauty salon: she's a hairdresser and he's a physio. They take home €4,000 between them. Harry receives a fee from the local football club, where he covers big matches. He expects €250 in November and €300 in December. They expect a bumper month in December and plan to take home €6,000 to have money for a holiday in January. Prepare their income budget for October, November and December.

EXPENSES

Household expenses can be classified, which helps to ensure we catch everything. We list the following:

- Fixed expenses
- Variable expenses
- Discretionary expenses
- Mystery items

You can classify expenses for your household or business any way you want, but I suggest the following because they help us to look behind the actual expenses and see how those expenses behave – how they change and increase or decrease over time.

Fixed expenses

Fixed expenses are items we have to pay and which are *fixed in time and amount.* They may be paid monthly, quarterly or yearly. They include such things as the mortgage or rent payments, loan repayments, motor tax, all insurances (life, house, motor, health) and pension contributions.

Variable expenses

Variable expenses are regular payments whose amounts vary from week to week (or month to month). Examples are all those bills that show up from time to time (monthly, bimonthly or quarterly) that we pay to continue our life and lifestyle: travel expenses to school and work, food and groceries, telephone, internet, TV, electricity, gas, oil, etc.

Discretionary expenses

Discretionary expenses are the normal, *but optional*, expenses we can increase, decrease or stop paying if we want to. This includes such things as savings, pocket money, entertainment (videos, take-away meals, drinks), birthdays, Christmas presents, holidays, music festivals, etc. When trouble hits, like when someone loses their job, these are the first things we look to cut because we can get immediate effect without too much pain. We can stop paying them if we have to.

Mystery items

There is a fourth classification never mentioned in the textbooks, until now: missing money. It applies only to household budgets (well, it applies to mine!). You know the story: you go to the ATM for your week's supply of cash and next thing you know, poof, it's gone! Newspaper: check. Bus fare: check. Drink after work with the girls: check. Eh, I'm missing €40. Oh yeah, taxi home €20: check … still short €20. You recite the day's activities. No good. It's just gone. Count your cash at bedtime and make sure you carry a spending notebook/card/piece of paper. Seriously, try it!

Allow for the fact that we spend money on bits and pieces, which we forget. It's just another heading in our budget, and the better we get at recordkeeping, the smaller it becomes. What results from the overall exercise, however, is a sharper awareness of what we actually spend our hard-earned cash on. Most, of course, is spent on good and proper things, but a seminar participant who ate a lot of meals on the go once said, 'I was amazed at how much good money I spend on bad food.'

LAYOUT RULES

Next, we have to get the layout right. Layout is important in all business documents dealing with financial matters – it either makes something easy to read and understand or complicates it horribly. Humour me while I set out a few basic rules for accounting/business/financial documents, everything from a simple handwritten invoice to a company's balance sheet:

1. All documents must have a title, e.g. Invoice, Budget.
2. The title should refer to the appropriate date or period, e.g. Budget for January 2014.

3. Documents usually begin at the top left of the page and end at the bottom right, so your answer or final figure, e.g. Invoice Total or Take-home Pay, should be at the bottom right of the document/report.
4. Present figures in neat columns, all right aligned.
5. All money columns should have a euro/currency sign just at the top, and none in the body of the document. Sometimes the final figure will be 'dressed' with a euro/currency sign, e.g. €40.00.

Let's look at a simple sample for expenses that follows these rules. We'll continue the income sample we used earlier for John and Alice Smith. After a couple of exercises, we'll combine the income and expenses and 'top and tail' the combination to give some really useful information.

Expenses budget for John and Alice Smith for 3 months ended 31 March			
EXPENSES	Jan	Feb	Mar	Total
	€	€	€	€
Fixed expenses:				
Mortgage	1,250	1,250	1,250	3,750
Car repayments	500	500	500	1,500
Insurances (1)	870		250	1,120
Variable expenses:				
Oil, gas, ESB (2)	600	600	500	1,700
TV, phone, internet	400	400	400	1,200
Groceries (2)	750	750	750	2,250
Discretionary payments:				
Pocket money	300	300	300	900
Entertainment	200	200	350	750
Birthdays, etc.				
Savings	200	200	200	600
Other	150	150	150	450
Total income (3)	5,220	4,350	4,650	14,220

Notes:

(1) Insurance is always paid upfront or in monthly instalments. So although it covers the whole year, we account for it when we pay the money. That way we know how much we spend in each month.

(2) Groceries often cause problems. They are variable, not fixed. Ask any household executive (Mam or Dad) how much they spend per week or month on groceries and they will give you a rough figure. It's always a hard figure to estimate accurately in most families because you do a 'big shop' perhaps once a week, but then you might have a milkman delivering milk, or you pop out to the corner shop for bread or a few carrots. If you're anything like me, this happens at least twice a week, every week. But overall you spend a similar amount each week/month on groceries. So although an exercise or exam question might say 'they spend €200 a week on groceries', this is still a variable, and not a fixed, expense. To be fixed it has to be fixed in time and amount, and grocery shopping isn't fixed in time. Similarly, bills like phone and heating vary every month, but for our purposes we usually estimate a standard monthly amount in the budget. Again it's variable, not fixed.

(3) Notice the single line above and below the total expenses. This becomes more important in the section on balances (below).

You can see that the layout matches exactly with the income budget on page 122: columns for each month and a total column; clear headings and narrations; and expenses are classified and listed, combining various expenses together where appropriate (otherwise the statement would have to be pages long and therefore hard to read). The mystery classification is discreetly tucked away as 'Other'. In real life you might call this 'Contingencies' or 'Unidentified Expenses'. **Contingencies** means expenses we haven't thought of or that we've forgotten. Also, there are things that haven't happened before, or maybe the family decides to buy a new kitchen. Remember, it's just a budget – nobody knows what's going to happen tomorrow, never mind next month or next year. But that doesn't stop us from planning for what we think might happen (like business improving a little as the economy grows) or for what we might want to happen (like the children convincing Dad to take us all to Disney World in Florida next year...). In a business, the managing director may have set ambitious targets for sales of a new product or in a new market and these will be built into the next year's budget.

When you do both the income and the expenses parts of a budget, the obvious question is, 'What happens to the difference between income and expenses?' In other words, we have to extend the layout to include what we call the net cash flow each month.

Cash flow is the word used to indicate the movement, or flow, of money. If we receive more than we pay out, we have a positive cash flow. If we pay out more than we take in, it's negative.

Net means small or neat in business and accounting circles. The opposite of net is **gross**. When you read about wages in Chapter 9, you saw that there was gross pay, and when we had deducted the taxes and other items, you were left with a much smaller net pay. In Chapter 13 we'll talk about gross and net profit. It's the same thing: a big version (gross profit) and after the deduction of expenses, a smaller version (net profit).

Data means what is given – the raw detail that we start with – such as the details given in a question, the invoices for a month, the number of customers in a shop hour by hour for a week or answers in a bundle of completed questionnaires.

Information is what we get when we analyse and summarise data into sensible segments or classifications. We have sorted data about income and expenses into monthly totals. Now we want to go further and see what we can learn. (Data and information also appear in Chapter 14.)

To add in net cash flow and a balance section, we need to calculate the net cash flow and insert the opening balance at the start of our budget period.

When you put the income and expenses sections on the same page, it's easy to subtract the expenses from the income to see what's left each month – the net cash flow. This is shown as A – B, or income minus expenses.

The balance is easy: we know what's in the bank today or have a fair idea what will be in the bank by next week or next month (whenever the budget period starts). Having inserted that into the layout, just add on any positive cash flow and deduct any negative cash flow to get an estimate of what we expect the bank balance will be at the end of each month of the period. We call this the **budgeted bank balance**.

Budget for John and Alice Smith for 3 Months Ended 31 March				
INCOME	Jan	Feb	Mar	Total
Salary: John	3,240	3,240	3,550	10,030
Alice	1,120	1,620	1,120	3,860
Bank interest	—	—	60	60
Other (art classes)	100	100	100	300
Total income (A)	4,460	4,960	4,830	14,250
EXPENSES				
Fixed expenses:				
Mortgage	1,250	1,250	1,250	3,750
Car repayments	500	500	500	1,500
Insurances	870		250	1,120
Variable expenses:				
Oil, gas, ESB	600	600	500	1,700
TV, phone, internet	400	400	400	1,200
Groceries	750	750	750	2,250
Discretionary expenses:				
Pocket money	300	300	300	900
Entertainment	200	200	350	750
Birthdays, etc.				
Savings	200	200	200	600
Other	150	150	150	450
Total expenses (B)	5,220	4,350	4,650	14,220
Net cash flow (A−B)	(760) (1)	610	180	30
Opening balance (2)	1,000	240 (3)	850 (3)	1,000 (2)
Closing balance	240	850	1,030 (4)	1,030 (4)

Notes:

(1) Notice that we use brackets to indicate minus or negative amounts in accounting statements and reports. One reason for this is that even a bad photocopy will clearly show a number in brackets, but a typed minus sign can be missed.

(2) Insert the opening bank balance *twice* because it's the opening bank balance for January and *also* for the whole period (i.e. total).

(3) The previous month's closing balance is this month's opening balance. Whatever is in your purse at the end of today (this period) is also in your purse at the start of tomorrow (next period).

(4) The last month's balance has to be the same as the Total column balance, because they both represent the closing balance on 31 March. You also know your tots are correct when these two agree.

EXERCISE 12.2

John and Kay Lahart earn €2,500 and €3,000 a month, respectively. They pay rent of €1,250 a month and car repayments of €750 a month. Their health insurance, €2,500 a year, falls due in March. They estimate grocery bills at €1,000 a month and gas and electricity bills of €350, paid in February and April. They save €1,000 a month in the credit union and they are planning a romantic trip to Paris in February, costing €2,500 all in. They currently have €500 in the bank. Prepare their budget for January to April.

READING A BUDGET

Let's look at the Morris family budget for a week as an example. Michael Morris earns €650 a week and his wife, Mary, has a part-time job, giving her a net €200 a week to take home. They have no other income. They have €850 in the bank today. They pay a mortgage of €300 a week and grocery bills amount to an average of €180 a week. Energy costs around €20 a week and the phone is estimated at €12 a week. Granny Morris minds their son, Martin, and they give her €40 a week for herself and for any small expenses. They put €120 in the credit union as savings and €40 into a holiday account. Prepare a family budget and show how much cash they expect to have left at the end of a typical week.

Weekly Budget for Michael and Mary Morris, January ← Title/Name/Date

€ ←

INCOME		
Michael	650	Currency sign
Mary	200 ←	
Total income	850 ←	Amounts, right justified
EXPENSES		
Fixed:		
Mortgage	300	
Variable:		
Energy bills	20	
Telephone and TV	12	Subtotals
Groceries	180	
Childminding	40	Headings for clarity
Discretionary:		
Savings	120	
Holiday account	40	
Total income	712 ←	
Net cash flow for the week	138	
Opening bank balance	850	
Closing bank balance	€988 ←	Currency sign for 'dressing' Double line to finish

Many people will look at this budget and say, 'So what? Does this tell me any-thing I didn't know already?' Well, perhaps not. But what if (a great question in budgeting) Mary was to lose her part-time job? Now the budget tells a valuable story. It shows where they are spending their money and where they can achieve quick savings. This will allow life to continue with as little disruption as possible, which is very important for parents of young children.

They already have €138 surplus per week, so that on its own covers more than half the loss. There is €120 going into savings, which can be reduced to cover the rest. More careful shopping can reduce the grocery bill or maybe Granny can make do with a few euros less, meaning that they can manage quite well without Mary's money. Mind you, holidays might be less glamorous this year and the savings plans will take a hit, at least while Mary looks for another job.

So you can see that a budget is a simple exercise in itself, but it's what it does for us that makes it such a valuable planning tool. It allows governments, schools or businesses to ask those 'what if' questions and see how they might cope with a changed situation.

EXERCISE 12.3

(a) Quentin and Roxanne Sullivan have one child, Tommy, for whom they receive Child Benefit of €240 a month. Quentin earns €3,200 a month and expects a raise of 5% in February. Roxanne is a successful self-employed business consultant and earns €6,000 a month. Their mortgage costs €2,000 a month. They drive expensive cars costing €1,200 in loan repayments and €600 in petrol each month. Their grocery bills amount to €1,250 a month and childminding is €800. Heating and telephone amount to €550 in January and €600 in March. They pay health insurance in March of €3,000 and plan a cruise in April costing €4,000. They have a pension plan costing €2,000 a month and Tommy's birthday party in January will cost €1,000 (only the best for our darling Tommy!). They spend an average of €700 a month on clothes. Their bank balance on New Year's Day is expected to be €10,000. Prepare the family budget for January to April.

(b) Una and Val Walker both work in a local factory earning €1,400 and €1,800 a month, respectively. They are both expecting raises of 4% in June. Una expects a bonus in May of around €500. They live in a rented apartment, paying €1,300 a month, and insurance of €300 is payable in July. Electricity costs €200 in May and €150 in July and they pay €160 a month between them on mobile phones. Travelling costs them €180 a month and they have lunch in the work canteen, costing €200 a month. Otherwise their pocket money is about €200 each per month. Groceries cost €600 a month and they save €500 a month in the credit union towards the cost of their first car. They have €600 in the bank today.

   (i) Prepare their budget for May, June and July.

   (ii) They plan to visit Una's sister near Rome in July, but they will need €1,400. Will they have enough for the trip?

   (iii) If not, what can they do to make it happen? Make three suggestions. Write a note on what you feel is the best one and state why.

BUSINESS BUDGETS

Business budgets are a bit more complex, but basically very similar to the household version we've already seen. The income and expenses headings are almost all different, of course, but the layout is identical and the purpose is also identical. Instead of salaries and Child Benefit, for income you'll have cash sales and debtors receipts, and instead of school bus fares, mortgage repayments and groceries, you'll see things like VAT and PAYE payments, corporation tax, bank charges, creditors payments and advertising. You'll also see the old chestnuts, just like at home: telephone, rent, insurance, motor and travel, repairs and loan repayments, but no savings, no birthdays, no holidays and no pocket money! There will be discretionary elements too, but they're harder to identify.

Can you think of a few business expenses that might be discretionary? How about advertising, or maybe sponsorship, charitable or political donations, overly expensive cars for the directors, excessive decor in some offices or corporate boxes at sports venues?

Businesses frequently show their monthly sales at the head of the monthly columns, as so many of the figures in the budget depend on, or vary with, the sales level planned for each month.

- Can you name some expenses that could be said to vary with sales volume? This could include purchases of product (if we sell it, we have to buy it or make it), wages, commissions, wrapping, delivery charges, etc.
- Can you name some expenses that won't vary and say why? This could include salary, rent, insurance, advertising (sales may vary with this one, not the other way round!), motor and travelling, rates/property, printing and stationery, to name just a few.

These expenses occur because we're in business. If we do well or not so well – whether we sell lots of goods or none – we still have to pay for printing, we still have to pay the directors and managers and we still have to pay our rent and rates. However, for the purposes of budgeting, it's useful to identify as many costs as possible that have a connection with the volume of sales each month. Then we can make our cost budgets change as we vary our expectation of sales for the coming months. These costs are called **variable costs**.

Just as in the household, in business we also have **fixed expenses**. However, we define them slightly differently as expenses that do not vary with the volume of sales.

Hopefully there are none of the mystery items (unrecorded expenses) in any business you know. Obviously, businesses have books and bookkeepers, computers and systems designed to make sure there are no spending gaps like the ones in my house!

EXERCISE 12.4

Niall and Orla Pye are about to start a small builders' providers business. They buy all their supplies from Leinster Suppliers and are allowed 2 months to pay. When they sell, they double the prices charged and sell everything on 1 month's credit (i.e. their debtors pay the month after they buy). They sold €10,000, €12,000 and €15,000 in the 3 months to 31 March. So they have to pay €5,000, €6,000 and €7,500 to Leinster Suppliers in March, April and May. They also received a VAT refund in February of €350. They pay 10% of sales each month as a commission, and delivery and other charges amount to 5% of sales. They pay themselves €800 each a month and they pay the following expenses: phone €100 a month, electricity and gas €200 in January and €350 in March. They pay PAYE of €1,000 in February and waste charges of €150 in March. Property tax of €200 has to be paid in January and other business expenses amount to €2,000 a month. Their opening bank balance on 1 January is €5,000. Prepare a budget for 3 months to 31 March.

CAR LOANS AND MORTGAGES

Sometimes we want to buy something big, like a car or a house. These are the two largest purchases most households make in a lifetime. A new car will tend to cost most of a year's earnings. Not many people can manage to save that amount of money easily, so we use borrowings, e.g. a car loan. A house will typically cost three or more times what any family can earn in a whole year. This needs even bigger borrowing and for a longer time: a mortgage.

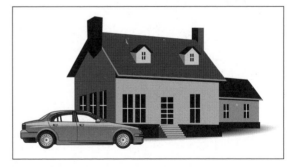

A lesson to note here is that when you have to borrow money for a major purchase, you usually won't be able to borrow for longer than the life of the thing you're buying. A car loan is usually for 5 years at most, which is the normal life of a car. After 5 years, it's not worth much! During the life of the loan it's **secured** by the car's value. If you can't pay the loan, the bank can take back the car and sell it to clear the balance.

Similarly, a mortgage on a house is usually for 20, 25 or even 30 years. But then, a house lasts a long time and usually holds its value (except when a crash happens, like in 2008/9 in Ireland). Under normal circumstances house values rise over time, and if you have to, you can sell the house and pay off the mortgage loan in the future. The loan is secured by the value of the house. Incidentally, a mortgage is just a particular type of contract where you can't sell the house without the bank's permission, but apart from that, it's just a long-term loan.

However, for the first time ever in Ireland, the property crash caused what is called **negative equity**. This means that although you borrowed a lot of money and the house was supposed to secure the loan, the crash caused the house value to fall below what you owe the bank and you can no longer clear the loan by selling the house. Ouch. This wasn't supposed to happen. In fairness, Ireland has never experienced negative equity before. Property values may have slowed or stayed the same for a few years in the past, but they had never fallen. This is the bad side of the Celtic Tiger, the name given to Ireland's booming economy during the years from the mid-1990s to 2008/9.

'People often ask me if I was funny as a child. I say, well, no, I was an accountant!'

—*Ellen DeGeneres*

'I'm working as hard as I can to get my life and my cash to run out on the same day.'

—*Doug Sanders*

Prices and Profit

A business buys goods and sells them at a profit. Simple. You do this over and over to make a living. To make more profit, you have to either sell the same amount of goods at a higher price or sell more goods at the same price. Your local grocery store tends to be rather expensive, but you pay because it's so handy. To save money, you go to one of the larger chain stores that sells more goods – way more goods – and therefore can sell at a lower price than the local store.

Remember, the profit you make by buying and selling, **gross profit**, has to do a lot of work. It has to pay:

- The wages of shop staff
- The costs of running the shop (electricity, cleaning, wrapping, insurance and rent)
- Advertising, bank interest, delivery charges
- The shop owner for their work and investment

When an owner is calculating their selling prices, he or she will normally have a standard formula they use: 'I must make x% on cost to make a living.' So when they receive a delivery of goods, they have to go over the prices they're paying to calculate the appropriate prices at which to sell each one. That's why something as simple as a bar of chocolate can be sold at several different prices in different shops on the same street.

Let's get the language straight first. Here's one arrangement looked at in two ways, bottom up and top down:

	€
Buy for	100
Add mark-up	50
Sell for	150
Percentage mark-up	50% on cost

	€
Sell for	150
Cost price	100
Profit	50
Percentage profit	33.3% on sales

If you can keep this simple example in mind, we'll all get along just fine. Try a few exercises.

EXERCISE 13.1

Calculate the mark-up and selling price.
(a) Buy for €1.50   Mark-up 40%
(b) Buy for €3.75   Mark-up 20%
(c) Buy for €12.50   Mark-up 60%
(d) Buy for €72.00   Mark-up 80%
(e) Buy for €1,200.00   Mark-up 125%

EXERCISE 13.2

Calculate the mark-up and the percentage of cost price.
(a) Buy for €1.20   Sell for €1.50
(b) Buy for €2.65   Sell for €3.71

(c) Buy for €36.00   Sell for €64.80

(d) Buy for €36.00   Sell for €75.60

(e) Buy for €165.00   Sell for €230.00

EXERCISE 13.3

Calculate the cost price.

(a) Sell for €4.50   Mark-up 25%

(b) Sell for €2.32   Mark-up 60%

(c) Sell for €59.40   Mark-up 35%

(d) ˙ Sell for €695.44   Mark-up 65%

(e) Sell for €4,112.50   Mark-up 75%

If you can master those, you have your head around mark-up. Now do the same in Exercise 13.4 for profit.

PROFIT

In this case, we're looking at **gross profit**. This is simply the difference between selling price and buying cost. It can also include other additional costs associated with the buying of the goods, but that's for another text!

EXERCISE 13.4

Calculate the gross profit amount and the percentage of sales.

(a) Buy for €1.50   Sell for €2.00

(b) Buy for €3.75   Sell for €7.50

(c) Buy for €12.50   Sell for €18.75

(d) Buy for €72.00   Sell for €160.00

(e) Buy for €1,200.00   Sell for €2,500.00

EXERCISE 13.5

Calculate the cost price and the percentage of gross profit to sales.

(a) Sell for €1.50   Gross profit €0.75

(b) Sell for €3.71   Gross profit €2.41

(c) Sell for €64.80   Gross profit €22.70

(d) Sell for €75.60   Gross profit €18.15

(e) Sell for €365.95   Gross profit €263.48

EXERCISE 13.6

Calculate the cost price and the selling price.

(a) Gross profit is €8.00 and 50% on sales

(b) Gross profit is €27.50 and 25% on sales

(c) Gross profit is €33.00 and 30% on sales

(d) Gross profit is €28.00 and 72% on sales

(e) Gross profit is €99.37 and 79.5% on sales

FOREIGN CURRENCY

When you go on holidays to Spain you bring euros with you and/or you use a credit card. You don't have any currency problems because Spain, like Ireland, uses the euro. But what if you go outside the eurozone? What if you go to America, the UK or Switzerland? These countries aren't in the eurozone, so you can't use euros there. The credit card is a great help here. If you use it, you just key in your PIN and the credit card company does the rest (the bill is paid and converted to euros on your next statement). No prob-lay-mo, as they say.

But you'll need cash for a London taxi, a bar of Swiss chocolate or a glass of Californian wine, so what do you do? You go to your bank and exchange your euros for an equivalent amount in dollars, pounds or Swiss francs. As of 1 January 2013 according to the foreign currency website www.xe.com, the exchange rates for €1 were:

- €1 = 1 American dollar and 31 cents ($1.31)
- €1 = 81 pence sterling (£0.81)
- €1 = 1 Swiss franc and 21 centimes (1.21 CHF)

You'll find daily quotes for the main world currencies in most newspapers. It will usually be in a box headed 'The Euro'. The rates shown mean how much you will get for one euro in that currency. If you're reading a British newspaper, such a box would read 'The Pound' because that paper's usual readers are British. Those rates will show how much you would get in each currency for one pound sterling.

Using the rates on page 138, how much of each currency will €300 buy for your holiday?

Dollars: €1 = $1.31   €300 × 1.31 = $393.00

Sterling: €1 = £0.81   €300 × 0.81 = £243.00

Swiss Francs: €1 = CHF 1.21   €300 × 1.21 = CHF 363.00

So you see, it's not difficult as long as you take your time and make sure to get the signs right, read the rate properly and multiply or divide as appropriate. Just write the rate out as €1 = xyz, just as I did above. Then check your calculation with a currency you know even slightly. For example, you might know that a dollar is worth less than a euro and that a pound is worth more than a euro, so use these to make sure you're multiplying or dividing properly. In your sample calculation, you should get a bigger number of dollars and a smaller number of pounds for your euros. If you then repeat the calculations using the rate for Thailand bats or Chinese yuan, you can trust your answer (because, I don't know about you, but I haven't a clue how much those currencies are worth!). Of course, you can use the www.xe.com website too, but will you have your laptop in your hand or have a guaranteed signal on your phone just when you see the perfect gift for your mam/boyfriend/favourite cousin on the way back from the beach in Egypt/Columbia/New Zealand?

EXERCISE 13.7

Calculate the amount in dollars, pounds and Swiss francs for each of the following amounts.

(a) €6.60

(b) €365.00

(c) €1,325.50

(d) €26,856.65

These rates have to be used differently if we reverse the above question: what's the equivalent in euros and cents of 300 US dollars, Swiss francs and pounds sterling?

US dollars: $300
€1 = $1.31
How many 1.31s are in $300? Divide: 300 ÷ 1.31 = €229.01

Pounds sterling: £300
€1 = £0.81
How many 81ps are in £300? Divide: 300 ÷ 0.81 = €370.37

Swiss francs: CHF 300
€1 = 1.21
How many 1.21s are in CHF 300? Divide: 300 ÷ 1.21 = €247.93

EXERCISE 13.8

Calculate the equivalent amount in euros and cents for the following currency amounts.

(a) £8.50

(b) £27.65

(c) £138.62

(d) £13,265.21

(e) $6.50

(f) $38.40

(g) $278.52

(h) $11,864.25

(i) CHF 4.32

(j) CHF 24.30

(k) CHF 365.44

(l) CHF 1,388.63

EXERCISE 13.9

(a) A leather armchair in your shop was bought six months ago from a New York design firm. You need to sell it! It is marked 'On Sale – 33% Off'. The new price is €350.

VAT on furniture is 23%. The shop has a policy of adding 50% to cost before VAT and the dollar was worth 85 cents the day you bought it.

(i)   What was the selling price before the sale?

(ii)   How much VAT did that include?

(iii)   How much profit were you originally expecting?

(iv)   What was the original cost price in euros and cents?

(v)   What was the dollar price?

(vi)   How much profit, if any, will you make if you sell it today for €350?

(b)   I bought some items in London and paid in sterling (pounds and pence). I converted to euros at €1 = £0.82. I added 45% mark-up and 23% VAT. Then I sold the items for €2,500.

(i)   What is the VAT-exclusive price?

(ii)   How much profit did I make?

(iii)   The mark-up was 45%. What is the percentage profit?

(iv)   What was the euro cost price?

(v)   How much did I pay in sterling?

'To become rich, rise early, work hard, strike oil.'

—J.P. Getty

'Money isn't the most important thing in life, but it's reasonably close to oxygen on the "gotta have it" scale.'

—Zig Ziglar

CHAPTER 14

Lies, Damned Lies and Statistics

There's a great word: statistics. Sta-tis-tics. Awkward to type, awkward to say. It got a BBC newsreader sacked one time because he couldn't pronounce it on air. Mark Twain, the American author, once said there were 'lies, damned lies and statistics', and the way some politicians and others use statistics, you'd have to agree.

Like so much of the maths in this book, we're already familiar with statistics. They're used every day in all sorts of situations, from the weather, to the football league, to record sales, to the biggest-grossing movie of all time.

Mícheál Ó Muircheartaigh, the much-loved Irish sports commentator, once said at a greyhound race meeting, 'No dog ever won this race twice, but one dog won it three times once.' On careful examination he's not quite accurate, but nonetheless, it's a great quote and it's statistics.

We are constantly comparing and grouping information to make a point: average age of the students in the class, average house prices, most goals in a season, most away wins, on average the boys are taller than the girls, and so on. Statistical information is gathered in all sorts of ways. We can carry out a survey by questioning people on the street about a product. We can observe the number of people walking into a shop between the hours of 9 and 11 each day or the number of passengers on the number 18 bus.

Let's start with some definitions.

- **Statistics** is the mathematics of gathering, analysing, interpreting and presenting large amounts of information.
- **Data** (from the Latin word 'to give', like 'donation') is individual pieces of given information, e.g. each boy's/girl's height, the price of each house, each sales invoice.

- **Quantitative data** is information about the number of things or events in a population.

- **Qualitative information** is about the type of data: things that can't be measured in numbers, like the senses, smell, colour, shape, etc. Sometimes you hear radio interviewers asking a quantitative question about a qualitative thing: 'How hard has it been to do xyz?' 'Oh, *very* hard' is the usual answer. Meaningless! But then you'll hear another interviewer ask, 'On a scale of one to ten, how hard has it been?' Now there's a much better question, because she has offered a measuring scale (one to ten). Now you can answer, 'Very hard – maybe eight.'

- **Primary information** is data collected directly, by any means, such as questionnaire or observation.

- **Secondary information** is the result of analysis, summary and presentation of primary data by others, usually from newspapers, journals or websites.

- A **census** is a collection of data about all the items in a set (such as the population of the country). The Central Statistics Office does this.

- A **survey** is a collection of data from a sample of a set.

- **Information** is what we get when we gather lots of data in some logical order.

- **Population** is all the items in a particular set, like all the boys in the class, or all the girls, or all the people in a country.

- **Random sampling** is a process of selecting a sample where, at every point, every item in the population has the possibility of being chosen. It's like a draw for a raffle, where someone dips their hand into a drum of tickets – any ticket could be drawn.

- **Average** is a single number representing an entire set of data. There are three types of average:

  - ➤ **Arithmetic mean** is what most of us are used to. It is a simple average, which is all the values added together and divided by the number of values. For example, there are 6 girls aged 14, 15, 15, 15, 17 and 17. The arithmetic mean is $\frac{93}{6} = 15\ ½$.

  - ➤ **Median** is the middle number in the set arranged in order – in this case, 15, or more accurately, 15 and 15. If there are two, you add them together and divide by 2. No problem here as both are the same, but that's not always the case.

  - ➤ **Mode** is the most common point in the set. In our case, there are three 15s and two 17s. 15 is the mode, or the modal point.

EXERCISE 14.1

Calculate/identify the mean, mode and median of each of the following groups of data (to one decimal place if necessary).

(a) 2, 2, 5, 6, 8, 8, 8, 9, 9, 10

(b) 14, 14, 15, 15, 15, 16, 17, 17, 17, 17

(c) 16, 8, 25, 64, 8, 7, 93, 10, 5, 5

(d) 12, 9, 23, 56, 58, 14, 15, 7, 40, 19

TABULATING DATA

I'm an accountant. **Tabulating data** is what bookkeepers do before accountants come along to process the information they produce. Let's look at a basic piece of data: an invoice.

Invoice No. 55 dated 31 January 2013
To John Murphy, 17 Main Street, Anytown

5 cotton shirts @ €20.00 each	100.00
VAT at 23%	23.00
Total	€123.00

There's your basic invoice. Then the bookkeeper tabulates it, with others, in the sales book like this:

Details	No.	Total	VAT	Shirts	Slacks	Socks
J Murphy	55	123	23	100		
P Nolan	56	246	46	50	130	20
M Mulcahy	57	123	23	50		50
		492	92	200	130	70

It's not hard to imagine this as a list with 40 or even 100 invoices listed and how useful that information would be for a manager looking at any week or month in any business. So from a bunch of invoices containing basic data, we can now see an ordered tabulation showing total values for all sales as well as the sales of shirts, slacks and socks and how much VAT they charged. Now *that's* information!

OK, enough accountancy. Suppose I look at the students in any school and tabulate how many do the different subjects. It might look like this:

Irish	//////////	10
English	////////	8
Maths	/////////////	13
Spanish	////	4
Science	///////	7
Polish	////	4

Now list them in order. This is called an **array** of data: it's an arrangement of data into ascending or descending order.

$$4, 4, 7, 8, 10, 13$$

That's six subjects, with 46 students in all.

The mean number of students per class is $46 \div 6 = 7.7$.

The mode, or most frequent number in a class, is 4.

The median number per class is $(7 + 8) \div 2 = 7.5$.

RANGE

A **range** of data is the highest value minus the lowest value. It shows the spread of data. The range of class sizes in the example above is $13 - 4 = 9$.

FREQUENCY TABLES

A **frequency table** is a table or chart showing how often a value or an event occurs in a population. The chart above showing the students in different classes is a frequency table.

If someone asks how long it takes me to cycle to and from work, I have to answer, 'About half an hour going in and a bit longer coming home.' My times are dictated by:

- How I'm feeling (rested, refreshed or lazy)
- How tired I am (after a long day, maybe)
- The weather (rain and wind or sunny and bright)

- The traffic
- The traffic lights
- The trains, which can delay me at a level crossing

The only way to accurately answer the question is to record my times over a period and work out the averages. On a good day I get to work in 27 or 28 minutes, but it might take 35. Coming home usually takes 35 minutes but may take 45. A further complication is that sometimes I get the bus. Rarely will this take less than an hour. But let's ignore the bus and look at 10 days' cycling times:

29 36 28 36 28 38 30 35 28 39 28 38 27 37 29 36 31 38 28 36

You'll notice that they are alternating between high and low, reflecting coming in and going home. I work hard to stay under 40 minutes coming home. I have my pride!

First tabulate the data:

27	/
28	/////
29	//
30	/
31	/
35	/
36	////
37	/
38	///
39	/

Now put the data in a frequency table.

Going in					Heading home				
27	28	29	30	31	35	36	37	38	39
1	5	2	1	1	1	4	1	3	1

This is really two frequency tables, going in and coming home, and two separate sets of data. So let's read them that way:

Mode: 28 and 36
Mean: 28.6 and 36.9

So the next time I'm asked the question, I can say that on average it takes me just over 28 ½ minutes going in and under 37 minutes coming home.

EXERCISE 14.2

Find the mean and mode of the following groups of data.

(a)   Number of interruptions in an office each morning for two weeks:

18, 20, 20, 19, 18, 18, 18, 20, 21, 18

(b)   Ages of children in a class:

7, 8, 8, 8, 9, 10, 10, 7, 7, 7, 8, 8, 9, 9, 9, 7

(c)   Answers given to one question on 24 questionnaires:

A, A, D, D, C, C, D, A, A, D, C, C, E, E, A, D, A, A, E, C, C, E, D, B

(d)   Ages of the customers in a hair salon on a Monday morning:

23, 28, 51, 41, 43, 52, 27, 73, 76, 41, 52, 50, 28, 35

(e)   Temperature at noon on each day of your holidays:

18, 18, 19, 20, 20, 22, 22, 24, 20, 21, 19, 22, 21, 22

SHOWING YOUR RESULTS VISUALLY

This is maths, but without (obvious) numbers. As so often in this book, you'll be familiar with this already. Look at the newspapers, especially around elections, which provide heaps of opportunities for graphic or pictorial representation.

We looked at a sales book earlier in the chapter, so let's take that idea and progress it a bit further. I asked you to imagine the sales book as it might look with 100 or more invoices. Well, if three invoices add up to just €500, then a month's sales with 100 invoices could easily be as much as €15,000 or more.

January	February	March	April	May	June
€15,000	€14,000	€16,000	€20,000	€22,000	€25,000

How would this look presented visually?

We have a few options, such as a graph, a bar chart or a pie chart. They will already be familiar to you, so let's see how to construct them.

The first is a plain **graph** with the time or months on the x axis and the monthly sales value on the y axis.

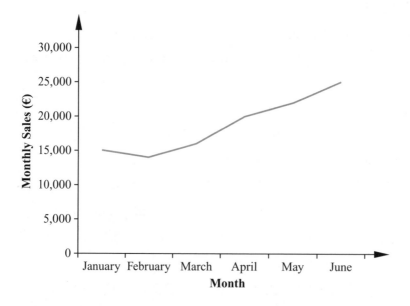

It's easy to read the value of sales each month. Even without reference to the value, you can see which months are best or worst over a period.

Here's the same information in a **bar chart**.

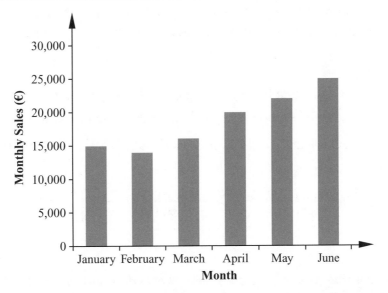

Again, it's easy to read and compare months. I particularly like bar charts because they're so easy to interpret. For example, we can see at a glance that June is almost twice as good as either February or March. You don't even have to see the numbers or do any maths.

Finally, there's a **pie chart**. This one is more pictorial and is used a lot in reports for consumption by laypeople, but it's not as easy (not for me, anyway) to compare the different elements.

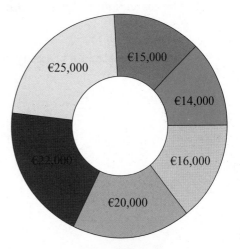

Here, each month looks like a slice of the six-month pie, or a doughnut, depending on which version you're using. The doughnut works better for me personally.

In the flat version it's easy to see that April, May and June are the better months, but not so easy to compare them in detail. You often see these in the newspaper after elections showing how the different political parties fill the seats in the Dáil.

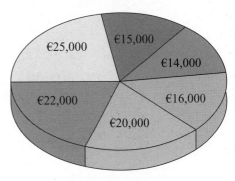

Creating a pie chart by hand is a bit technical and requires dividing the angles to be accurate. However, we're spoiled by technology – these three charts can all be produced using any modern spreadsheet program with a chart feature.

EXERCISE 14.3

Draw a bar chart **and** a graph representing the following data sets.

(a)   The early retirement group near my home has 15 members, aged:

61, 63, 61, 65, 65, 64, 66, 65, 64, 62, 63, 63, 66, 65, 66

(b)   My brother's last 20 golf scores last year were:

82, 85, 79, 80, 80, 90, 85, 78, 75, 78, 79,
81, 78, 76, 80, 82, 80, 82, 78, 80

'Statistics: the only science that allows different experts using the same figures to draw different conclusions.'

—Evan Esar

'A single death is a tragedy; a million deaths is a statistic.'

— Joseph Stalin

Indices and Logs

Indices is the plural of index. It's not a word you'll use very often. An **index** a small number written at the top right of another number to show it is multiplied by itself that many times. We can also use the word **exponent** instead of index. So what's *that* all about?

10^2 is 10 multiplied by itself, that is, two 10s multiplied together:

$$\underbrace{10 \times 10} \searrow 100$$

So 10^3 is three 10s multiplied together:

$$\underbrace{10 \times 10 \times 10} \searrow 1,000$$

When talking about and working with tens, watch the zeros and it's easy. We come across indices when looking at area or volume. Area is generally represented as square metres, or m^2, meaning we have multiplied one length in metres by another length in metres, and metres by metres is metres squared, or m^2 (a flat shape).

When looking at volume, we represent the answer as m^3, or metres cubed. This means that we have three amounts in metres multiplied together: the length, depth and height (a three-dimensional solid). For more specifics on this topic, refer to Chapter 8 on measurement.

Anyway, in this kind of maths – like in algebra, when we use letters to represent numbers – we don't use the multiply sign. So $p \times p \times p$ would be written ppp or p^3 and $a \times b$ is written ab.

But $p \times p \times p \times p$, or p^4, could be multiplied by $p \times p \times p$, or p^3. So that's p^4p^3. Writing it out the long way, as a multiplication, we would have:

$$p \times p \times p \times p \quad \times \quad p \times p \times p$$

Counting the Ps, this is p^7. That could also be achieved by simply adding the indices of the original numbers:

$$p^4 \times p^3 = p^{(4+3)}$$
$$\rightarrow p^7$$

THE EIGHT LAWS OF INDICES (OR MAYBE NINE)

This sounds much worse than it is. Laws sound serious, whereas they're really just operating rules. But let's have a look at them briefly and explain a little as we go.

More language: as if index and exponent weren't enough, when we have a number to an index, we usually speak it by saying 'to the power'. So 2^8 is described as 'two to the power eight' or sometimes 'to the power of eight'.

1. Any number to the power 0 is 1, e.g. $18^0 = 1$.

2. Any number to the power 1 equals itself, e.g. $b^1 = b$.

3. A number to the power -1 is its inverse, e.g. $b^{-1} = \frac{1}{b}$.

To explain these, let's look at a natural sequence of powers (watch 2, 1, 0, $-1, -2$):

$$7^2 = 1 \times 7 \times 7 = 49$$
$$7^1 = 1 \times 7 = 7$$
$$7^0 = 1 = 1$$
$$7^{-1} = 1 \div 7 = .1428$$
$$7^{-2} = 1 \div 7 \div 7 = .0204$$

4. To multiply powers of the same number, add the indices, e.g. $b^n \times b^m = b^{n+m}$. We saw this above in the Ps example.

5. To divide powers of the same number, subtract the indices, e.g. $b^n \div b^m = b^{n-m}$. If it works for multiplication, reverse it for division. It's the Ps again!

6. To raise a power to a power, multiply the indices, e.g. $(b^2)^3 = b^{(2\times3)} = b^6$. There's a funny explanation on www.mathsisfun.com. They give the example $(x^3)^4 = (xxx)(xxx)(xxx)(xxx) = xxxxxxxxxxxx = x^{12}$, so $(x^3)^4 = x^{3\times4} = x^{12}$.

7. To raise a multiplication expression to a power, raise each term in the expression to the power, e.g. $(ab)^n = a^n b^n$. Using the same logic as the last law, then this expression is $(ab)^4 = (ab)(ab)(ab)(ab) = aaaabbbb = a^4 b^4$, which is exactly what it says on the tin.

8. To raise a division expression to a power, raise each term in the expression to the power, e.g. $\left(\frac{a}{b}\right)^n = \frac{a^n}{b^n}$. If you can do it for multiplication, you can do it for division!

   Some folks include the following as an extra rule:

9. The number 1 raised to any power is always 1, e.g. $1^n = 1$. How hard can this one be: $1 \times 1 \times 1 \times 1 \times 1 = 1$. 'Nuff said!

LOGARITHMS (LOGS)

When you're working with indices, you're in the world of **logs** (I'm going to stick with the short form). Here's a definition I learned in school: if one number can be expressed as another number to an index, the log of the first number, to the base of the second, is the index.

Let's try it:

One number can be expressed as another number to an index: $8 = 2^3$
The log of the first number: that's 8
To the base of the second: that's 2
Is the index: that's 3

Put it all together and you get:

$$\log_2 8 = 3$$

'log eight, to the base two, is three'

However, **common logs** are to the base 10. These aren't so relevant to you and me today, because you have calculators. But before we had calculators, and that's not that long ago, we used logs when dealing with the multiplication and division of big numbers. We all owned a booklet of log tables. These were ready-calculated lists of hundreds of numbers (to four decimal places) that allowed us to make up the specific number we wanted. Look up ready reckoners or log tables online and see what they were. A log table was just a particular ready reckoner with a pre-calculated list of numbers – very specific numbers – indices, to be exact. The joy of all school-children … not!

Rules of logs

We have reviewed the laws of indices above. Well, if logs are really just indices of numbers, then the rules of logs are likely to have a familiar feel – and so they do. See how many you can connect.

1. The log of 1 to any base is 0:

$$\log 1 = 0$$

Incidentally, you should note that when you see 'log x', as I have written here, it assumes the base 10. These are called common logs.

2. The log of any number to the base of itself is 1:

$$\log_{10} 10 = 1$$

3. Product rule: The log of a multiplication, such as ab, is the log a plus log b:

$$\log(ab) = \log a + \log b$$

4. Quotient rule: Similarly, the log of a division, such as $\frac{a}{b}$, is the difference between log a and log b:

$$\log\left(\frac{a}{b}\right) = \log a - \log b$$

5. Power rule: The log of a number raised to a power is the power times the log of the number:

$$\log(a^b) = b \log a$$

6. Base change rule: The log of a number to a base is equal to the log of the number divided by the log of the base, both to a common base:

$$\log_b(a) = \frac{\log_x a}{\log_x b}$$

This base change rule is especially useful if you need to use a calculator, because calculators tend to use the base 10 as standard. So if you wanted to calculate $\log_9 3$, you simply change the base using the rule like this:

$$\log_9 3 = \log 3 \div \log 3 \text{ (both to base 10)}$$

EXERCISE 15.1

(a) Write the following in log form.
   (i) $3^2 = 9$
   (ii) $2^3 = 8$
   (iii) $3^5 = 243$

(b) Write the following in exponential (index) form.

   (i) $\log_3 81 = 4$

   (ii) $\log_2 32 = 5$

   (iii) $\log_3 27 = 3$

(c) What is the value of x in the following?

   (i) $\log_3 x = 4$

   (ii) $\log_3 9 = x$

   (iii) $\log_x 25 = 2$

(d) Write these as logs to base x.

   (i) $\log_k(m)$

   (ii) $\log_2(7)$

(e) Expand these.

   (i) $\log_a(xy)$

   (ii) $\log_a\left(\frac{2}{3}\right)$

   (iii) $\log_a(5^2)$

(f) Write these as single logs.

   (i) $\log x + 2\log y$

   (ii) $2\log x - 3\log y$

'Love is anterior to life, posterior to death, initial of creation, and the exponent of breath.'

—Emily Dickenson

Appendix

Tax Deduction Card

Revenue
Cáin agus Custaim na hÉireann
Irish Tax and Customs

EMPLOYEE'S DETAILS

Employee's Name

Employee's Address

PPS Number

Total Tax Credit

Total Cut-Off Point

Works Payroll No.

Tax Rate 1

Tax Rate 2

Tax Year

EMPLOYER'S DETAILS

Employer's Name

Employer's Number

PRSI CLASS

If PRSI Class changed during this employment complete these boxes

Initial PRSI Class

Date of Change   D D M M Y Y

Other Class   Weeks at Other Class

N.B. If more than two classes please furnish details on Form PRC1
If employment began (a) in Week 1 or later or (b) before Week 1 but the first pay day was in Week 1 or later, enter date of commencement.
If employment ceased during the tax year enter date of cessation.

Date of Commencement   D D M M Y Y

Date of Cessation   D D M M Y Y

Calculate   Click here if Week 1 Basis   New   Save As   Print
Calculate Week 1

Week	Date of Payment (DD/MM/YY)	Gross Pay (Less Superannuation) this period	Cumulative Gross Pay to Date	Cumulative Cut-Off Point	Cumulative Tax Due at Tax Rate 1	Cumulative Tax Due at Tax Rate 2	Cumulative Gross Tax	Cumulative Tax Credit Weekly	Cumulative Tax (Cannot be less than 0)	Tax Deducted this Period	Tax Refunded this Period	USC Deducted this Period	USC Refunded this Period	PRSI Weekly Record Insurable Employment	PRSI Class	PRSI Employee's Share	Total PRSI	Net Pay
1																		
2																		
3																		
4																		
5																		

Calculate   Click here if Week 1 Basis   New   Save As   Print
Calculate Week 1

RPC0746WHT_EN_WEL_2

This page may be photocopied for students' use.

Tax Deduction Card - Blank Sample

Employee Name:			PPS Number:			Tax Credit	€3,300 Total Cut-off	€32,000						

	G	H	I	J	K	L	M	N	O	P	Q	C	D	E	
Wk No	Gross Pay Less Superannuation	Cumulative Gross Pay to Date	Cumulative Standard Rate Cut-off point	Cumulative Tax Due at Standard Rate	Cumulative Tax Due at Higher Rate	Cumulative Gross Tax	Cumulative Tax Credit	Cumulative Tax (Cannot Be Less than 0)	Tax Deducted This Period	Tax Refunded This Period	Total USC	PRSI (ee)	PRSI Total	For Employers Use	PRSI Class
1			615.38				63.46								
2			1,230.76				126.92								
3			1,846.14				190.38								
4			2,461.52				253.85								
5			3,076.90				317.31								
6			3,692.28				380.77								
7			4,307.66				444.23								
8			4,923.04				507.69								
9			5,538.42				571.15								
10			6,153.80				634.62								
11			6,769.18				698.08								
12			7,384.56				761.54								
13			7,999.94				825.00								
14			8,615.32				888.46								
15			9,230.70				951.92								
16			9,846.08				1,015.38								
17			10,461.46				1,078.85								
18			11,076.84				1,142.31								
19			11,692.22				1,205.77								
20			12,307.60				1,269.23								
21			12,922.98				1,332.69								
22			13,538.36				1,396.15								
23			14,153.74				1,459.62								
24			14,769.12				1,523.08								
25			15,384.50				1,586.54								
26			15,999.88				1,650.00								

This sample shows just 26 weeks (half a year).

Tax Deduction Card Sample 1

				20%	41%				

Employee Name | PPS Number | Tax Credit | 3120 Total Cut-off

Wk No	G Gross Pay Less Superannuation	H Cumulative Gross Pay to Date	I Cumulative Standard Rate Cut-off point	J Cumulative Tax Due at Standard Rate	K Cumulative Tax Due at Higher Rate	L Cumulative Gross Tax	M Cumulative Tax Credit	N Cumulative Tax (Cannot Be Less than 0)	O Tax Deducted This Period	P Tax Refunded This Period
1	500.00		0.00	0.00	0.00		60.00			
2	500.00		0.00				120.00			
3	750.00		0.00				180.00			
4	300.00		0.00				240.00			
5			0.00				300.00			
6			0.00				360.00			
7			0.00				420.00			
8			0.00				480.00			
9			0.00				540.00			
10			0.00				600.00			
11			0.00				660.00			
12			0.00				720.00			
13			0.00				780.00			
14			0.00				840.00			
15			0.00				900.00			
16			0.00				960.00			
17			0.00				1,020.00			
18			0.00				1,080.00			
19			0.00				1,140.00			
20			0.00				1,200.00			
21			0.00				1,260.00			
22			0.00				1,320.00			
23			0.00				1,380.00			
24			0.00				1,440.00			
25			0.00				1,500.00			
26			0.00				1,560.00			

This sample shows just 26 weeks (half a year) without columns for PRSI or USC.

Tax Deduction Card Sample 1 — Completed

	20%	41%

Employee Name   PPS Number   Tax Credit   3120 Total Cut-off

Wk No	G Gross Pay Less Superannuation	H Cumulative Gross Pay to Date	I Cumulative Standard Rate Cut-off Point	J Cumulative Tax Due at Standard Rate	K Cumulative Tax Due at Higher Rate	L Cumulative Gross Tax	M Cumulative Tax Credit	N Cumulative Tax (Cannot Be Less than 0)	O Tax Deducted This Period	P Tax Refunded This Period
1	500.00	500.00	0.00	100.00	0.00	100.00	60.00	40.00	40.00	
2	500.00	1,000.00	0.00	200.00	0.00	200.00	120.00	80.00	40.00	
3	750.00	1,750.00	0.00	350.00	0.00	350.00	180.00	170.00	90.00	
4	300.00	2,050.00	0.00	410.00	0.00	410.00	240.00	170.00	---	
5			0.00				300.00			
6			0.00				360.00			
7			0.00				420.00			
8			0.00				480.00			
9			0.00				540.00			
10			0.00				600.00			
11			0.00				660.00			
12			0.00				720.00			
13	Do each week on its own, as you would in business.									
14										
15	Write neatly and always show 'zero, zero' for round euros (i.e 20.00, not 20).									
16										
17	When nil is the amount, write a generous dash, as in column O.									
18										
19	When starting a new card, carry forward the first and last cumulative amounts									
20	(Cumulative Gross Pay and Cumulative Tax).									
21										
22										
23	Never use a € sign. There's no room!									
24			0.00				1,440.00			
25			0.00				1,500.00			
26			0.00				1,560.00			

This sample shows just 26 weeks (half a year) without columns for PRSI or USC.

Tax Deduction Card Sample 2

Employee Name				PPS Number			Tax Credit 3,120	Total Cut-off 26,000	
	G	H	I	J	K	L	M	N	O	P
Wk No	Gross Pay Less Superannuation	Cumulative Gross Pay to Date	Cumulative Standard Rate Cut-off Point	Cumulative Tax Due at Standard Rate	Cumulative Tax Due at Higher Rate	Cumulative Gross Tax	Cumulative Tax Credit	Cumulative Tax (Cannot Be Less than 0)	Tax Deducted This Period	Tax Refunded This Period
1			500.00				60.00			
2			1,000.00				120.00			
3			1,500.00				180.00			
4			2,000.00		From old card		240.00			
5	700.00		2,500.00				300.00			
6	775.00		3,000.00				360.00			
7	805.00		3,500.00				420.00			
8	400.00		4,000.00				480.00			
9	700.00		4,500.00				540.00			
10			5,000.00				600.00			
11			5,500.00				660.00			
12			6,000.00				720.00			
13			6,500.00				780.00			
14			7,000.00				840.00			
15			7,500.00				900.00			
16			8,000.00				960.00			
17			8,500.00				1,020.00			
18			9,000.00				1,080.00			
19			9,500.00				1,140.00			
20			10,000.00				1,200.00			
21			10,500.00				1,260.00			
22			11,000.00				1,320.00			
23			11,500.00				1,380.00			
24			12,000.00				1,440.00			
25			12,500.00				1,500.00			
26			13,000.00				1,560.00			

This sample shows just 26 weeks (half a year) without columns for PRSI or USC.

Tax Deduction Card Sample 2 — Completed

	Employee Name		PPS Number				Tax Credit	3,120	Total Cut-off	26,000
Wk No	G Gross Pay Less Superannuation	H Cumulative Gross Pay to Date	I Cumulative Standard Rate Cut-off Point	J Cumulative Tax Due at Standard Rate	K Cumulative Tax Due at Higher Rate	L Cumulative Gross Tax	M Cumulative Tax Credit	N Cumulative Tax (Cannot Be Less than 0)	O Tax Deducted This Period	P Tax Refunded This Period
1			500.00				60.00			
2			1,000.00				120.00			
3			1,500.00				180.00			
4		2,050.00	2,000.00	From old card			240.00	170.00		
5	700.00	2,750.00	2,500.00	500.00	102.50	602.50	300.00	302.50	132.50	
6	775.00	3,525.00	3,000.00	600.00	215.25	815.25	360.00	455.25	152.75	
7	805.00	4,330.00	3,500.00	700.00	340.30	1,040.30	420.00	620.30	165.05	
8	400.00	4,730.00	4,000.00	800.00	299.30	1,099.30	480.00	619.30		1.00
9	700.00	5,430.00	4,500.00	900.00	381.30	1,281.30	540.00	741.30	122.00	
10			5,000.00				600.00			
11			5,500.00				660.00			
12			6,000.00				720.00			
13			6,500.00				780.00			
14			7,000.00				840.00			
15	As before, do each week on its own.									
16										
17	Remember, write neatly and always show 'zero, zero' and 'dash' for a nil amount.									
18										
19	When bringing forward amounts from an old card, bring the first and last cumulatives (Cumulative Gross Pay and									
20	Cumulative Tax) and insert in the appropriate boxes, highlighted here for illustration only. Then proceed exactly as before.									
21										
22										
23	Note that when a refund is the result, you put the figure in a separate 'Refund' column.									
24	Feel free to use weeks 10 to 14 to practise.									
25										
26		13,000.00					1,560.00			

This page may be photocopied for students' use.

Tax Deduction Card Sample 3

| Employee Name: | | PPS Number: | | | | | Tax Credit €3,825 | Total Cut-off €41,200 | | | | | | | |

Wk No	G Gross Pay Less Superannuation	H Cumulative Gross Pay to Date	I Cumulative Standard Rate Cut-off Point	J Cumulative Tax Due at Standard Rate	K Cumulative Tax Due at Higher Rate	L Cumulative Gross Tax	M Cumulative Tax Credit	N Cumulative Tax (Cannot Be Less than 0)	O Tax Deducted This Period	P Tax Refunded This Period	Q Total USC	C PRSI (ee)	D PRSI Total	E For Employers Use	PRSI Class
1			792.31				73.56								
2			1,584.62				147.12								
3			2,376.93				220.68								
4			3,169.24				294.24								
5			3,961.55				367.80								
6			4,753.86				441.36								
7			5,546.17				514.92								
8			6,338.48				588.48								
9			7,130.79				662.04								
10			7,923.10				735.60								
11			8,715.41				809.16								
12			9,507.72				882.72								
13			10,300.03				956.28								
14			11,092.34				1,029.84								
15			11,884.65				1,103.40								
16			12,676.96				1,176.96								
17			13,469.27				1,250.52								
18			14,261.58				1,324.08								
19			15,053.89				1,397.64								
20			15,846.20				1,471.20								
21			16,638.51				1,544.76								
22			17,430.82				1,618.32								
23			18,223.13				1,691.88								
24			19,015.44				1,765.44								
25			19,807.75				1,839.00								
26			20,600.06				1,912.56								

This sample shows just 26 weeks (half a year).

Universal Social Charge (USC) Payroll Card

This page may be photocopied for students' use.

Example 1 – Cumulative basis / standard rates

Weekly paid employee

P2C advises:

Cumulative Basis – effective from 1 January 2012

Rates of USC	
USC Rate 1	2%
USC Rate 2	4%
USC Rate 3	7%

	Weekly COP
USC Rate 1 Cut-off Point	193.00
USC Rate 2 Cut-off Point	308.00

Employer Payroll (USC)

Week No.	Gross Pay for USC (This Week)	Cumulative Gross Pay for USC to Date	Cumulative USC COP 1 (2%)	Cumulative USC Due at Rate 1 (2%)	Cumulative USC COP 2 (4%)	Cumulative USC Due at Rate 2 (4%)	Amount of Pay Chargeable at 7%	Cumulative USC Due at Rate 3 (7%)	Cumulative USC	USC Deducted This Period	USC Refunded This Period
1	250.00	250.00	193.00	3.86	308.00	* 2.28	0.00	0.00	6.14	6.14	0.00
2	250.00	500.00	386.00	7.72	616.00	4.56	0.00	0.00	12.28	6.14	0.00
3	475.00	975.00	579.00	11.58	924.00	13.80	51.00	3.57	28.95	16.67	0.00
4	250.00	1,225.00	772.00	15.44	1,232.00	18.12	0.00	0.00	33.56	4.61	0.00

* (250.00 – 193.00) @ 4%

The employee was absent on sick leave in weeks 5 and 6 and did not receive any pay. (Illness Benefit is not chargeable to USC.)

Week No.	Gross Pay for USC (This Week)	Cumulative Gross Pay for USC to Date	Cumulative USC COP 1 (2%)	Cumulative USC Due at Rate 1 (2%)	Cumulative USC COP 2 (4%)	Cumulative USC Due at Rate 2 (4%)	Amount of Pay Chargeable at 7%	Cumulative USC Due at Rate 3 (7%)	Cumulative USC	USC Deducted This Period	USC Refunded This Period
5	0.00	1,225.00	965.00	19.30	1,540.00	10.40	0.00	0.00	29.70	0.00	3.86
6	0.00	1,225.00	1,158.00	23.16	1,848.00	2.68	0.00	0.00	25.84	0.00	3.86
7	250.00	1,475.00	1,351.00	27.02	2,156.00	4.96	0.00	0.00	31.98	6.14	0.00
8	250.00	1,725.00	1,544.00	30.88	2,464.00	7.24	0.00	0.00	38.12	6.14	0.00
...											

Answers

EXERCISE 3.1
a 6
b 9
c 8
d 7
e 8
f 10
g 11
h 12
i 12
j 11
k 14
l 13
m 13
n 15
o 14

EXERCISE 3.2
a 43
b 117
c 198
d 1,399
e 2,122
f 6,010
g 1,949

EXERCISE 3.3
a 5
b 4
c 10
d 13

e 6
f 5
g 5
h 4

EXERCISE 3.4
a 29
b 65
c 38
d 18
e 17
f 27

EXERCISE 3.5
a 29
b 97
c 427
d 992
e 9,867
f 2,674
g 6,787
h 149,450

EXERCISE 3.6
a 69
b 168
c 215
d 762
e 1,896
f 7,758

EXERCISE 3.7

a
```
     23
   × 38
    184   23 × 8
    690   23 × 30
    874
```

b
```
      324
   ×  723
    1,296   324 × 3
    6,480   324 × 20
  226,800   324 × 700
  234,576
```

c
```
      643
   ×  562
    1,286   643 × 2
   38,580   643 × 60
  321,500   643 × 500
  361,366
```

d
```
    1,127
   ×   65
    5,635   1,127 × 5
   67,620   1,127 × 60
   73,255
```

e
```
      3,237
   ×    875
     12,948   3,237 × 5
    226,590   3,237 × 70
  2,589,600   3,237 × 800
  2,829,138
```

f
```
      3,862
   ×    629
     34,758   3,862 × 9
     77,240   3,862 × 20
  2,317,200   3,862 × 600
  2,429,198
```

EXERCISE 3.8

a 137

b 247

c 253

d 858

e 349

f 392

g 1,153

h 2,573

EXERCISE 3.9

a
```
          6 8
  2 4 | 1 6 3 2
        1 4 4
        1 9 2
        1 9 2
        ─
```

b
```
          8 9
  3 1 | 2 7 5 9
        2 4 8
        2 7 9
        2 7 9
        ─
```

c
```
          2 7 4
  1 6 | 4 3 8 4
        3 2
        1 1 8
        1 1 2
            6 4
            6 4
            ─
```

d
```
            7 6 8
  2 7 | 2 0 7 3 6
        1 8 9
        1 8 3
        1 6 2
            2 1 6
            2 1 6
            ─
```

e

```
              3 9 4
1 7 4 ⌐6 8 5 5 6
      5 2 2
      1 6 3 5
      1 5 6 6
          6 9 6
          6 9 6
          ─
```

f

```
                6 2 7
2 8 5 ⌐1 7 8 6 9 5
        1 7 1 0
          7 6 9
          5 7 0
          1 9 9 5
          1 9 9 5
          ─
```

EXERCISE 3.10

a $128 \, {}^{14}\!/_{17}$

b $374 \, {}^{16}\!/_{21}$

c $423 \, {}^{9}\!/_{18}$ or $423 \, \frac{1}{2}$

d $161 \, {}^{35}\!/_{65}$ or $161 \, {}^{7}\!/_{13}$

Note: It's always better to simplify fractions.

EXERCISE 4.1

a $x = 3y - 1$

b $x = 16 - 4y$

c $x = \dfrac{5y}{2}$

d $x = \dfrac{y + 10}{3} - y$

e $6x - 4x = 13 - 9$

EXERCISE 4.2 AND 4.3

a $x = 3, y = 1$

b $x = 2, y = 2$

c $x = 4, y = -1$

d $x = 4, y = 7$

e $x = 2, y = 2$

f $x = -3, y = 3$

EXERCISE 4.4 AND 4.5 (SAME PROBLEMS, SAME ANSWERS!)

a $(x + 1), (x + 2)$

b $(x - 5), (x - 1)$

c $(x - 5), (x - 3)$

d $(x - 6), (x + 5)$

e $(2x - 4), (x + 1)$

EXERCISE 4.6

a $a > 3$

b $b < 4$

c $x < 6$

d $y < 2$

e $x > 3$

f $a < 1$

EXERCISE 5.1

a $\dfrac{4}{5}$

b $\dfrac{5}{7}$

c $\dfrac{7}{8}$

d $\dfrac{9}{11}$

e $\dfrac{14}{15}$

f $\dfrac{11}{17}$

g $\dfrac{12}{15}$

h $\dfrac{71}{75}$

EXERCISE 5.2

a $\dfrac{3}{6} = \dfrac{1}{2}$

b $\dfrac{4}{8} = \dfrac{1}{2}$

c $\dfrac{4}{9}$

d $\dfrac{3}{11}$

e $\dfrac{6}{13}$

f $\dfrac{3}{15} = \dfrac{1}{5}$

EXERCISE 5.3

a $\frac{9}{27}$

b $\frac{17}{56}$

c $\frac{43}{65}$

d $\frac{106}{132} = \frac{53}{66}$

EXERCISE 5.4

a $\frac{3}{8}$

b $\frac{14}{12}$

c $\frac{17}{20}$

d $\frac{17}{21}$

e $\frac{11}{30}$

f $\frac{20}{21}$

EXERCISE 5.5

a $\frac{3}{12} = \frac{1}{4}$

b $\frac{28}{40} = \frac{7}{10}$

c $\frac{10}{24} = \frac{5}{12}$

d $\frac{14}{108} = \frac{7}{54}$

e $\frac{180}{272} = \frac{90}{136} = \frac{45}{68}$

EXERCISE 5.6

a $\frac{2}{3} \times \frac{4}{3} = \frac{8}{9}$

b $\frac{4}{5} \times \frac{8}{7} = \frac{32}{35}$

c $\frac{3}{4} \times \frac{5}{2} = \frac{15}{8}$

d $\frac{7}{8} \times \frac{6}{5} = \frac{42}{40} = \frac{21}{20}$

EXERCISE 5.7

a $\frac{7}{4}$

b $\frac{9}{4}$

c $\frac{7}{2}$

d $\frac{31}{4}$

e $\frac{43}{3}$

f $\frac{26}{3}$

g $\frac{82}{5}$

h $\frac{137}{7}$

EXERCISE 5.8

a a × b $\frac{7}{4} \times \frac{9}{4} = \frac{63}{16}$

b d × b $\frac{31}{4} \times \frac{9}{4} = \frac{279}{16}$

c a × e $\frac{7}{4} \times \frac{43}{3} = \frac{301}{12}$

d d × f $\frac{31}{4} \times \frac{26}{3} = \frac{806}{12} = \frac{403}{6}$

e c ÷ a $\frac{7}{2} \div \frac{7}{4} = \frac{7}{2} \times \frac{4}{7} = \frac{4}{2} = \frac{2}{1}$

f d ÷ b $\frac{31}{4} \div \frac{9}{4} = \frac{31}{4} \times \frac{4}{9} = \frac{31}{9}$

g h ÷ c $\frac{137}{7} \div \frac{7}{2} = \frac{137}{7} \times \frac{2}{7} = \frac{274}{49}$

h g ÷ f $\frac{82}{5} \div \frac{26}{3} = \frac{82}{5} \times \frac{3}{26}$

$= \frac{41}{5} \times \frac{3}{13} = \frac{123}{65}$

EXERCISE 6.1

a One point five (or perhaps point five zero, although final zeros can be ignored)

b Twelve point six zero four (sometimes we say O, as in the letter O, instead of zero, so you could also say twelve point six oh four)

c Three hundred and fifty-six point eight (ignoring the final zeros)

d Five thousand, six hundred and seventy-eight point zero seven six five

EXERCISE 6.2

a   3.45

b   44.078

c   567.005

d   1,282.5505

EXERCISE 6.3

a   1.4

b   1.6

c   1.9

d   1.8

e   1.350

f   1.639

g   1.950

h   1.125

EXERCISE 6.4

a   1.3

b   4.7

c   14.99

d   81.24

e   17.2002

f   262.549

g   703.18

EXERCISE 6.5

a   1.5

b   12.446

c   108.466

d   1,055.498

EXERCISE 6.6

a   0.1

b   2.15

c   11.69

d   9.467

e   115.2148

f   438.85

EXERCISE 6.7

a   12,345.6

b   3,908.65

c   12,340

d   22,560

e   67,600.2

f   32

EXERCISE 6.8

a   8.51

b   22.68

c   32.172

d   816.9664

e   1,230.63

f   0.2912

EXERCISE 6.9

a   1.256

b   0.59725

c   6.93872

d   2.5863

e   0.3657

f   0.00136

EXERCISE 7.1

a   33.3%

b   60.0%

c   87.5%

d   6.3%

e   142.9%

f   255.6%

EXERCISE 7.2

a 48%

b 65%

c 95%

d 134%

e 275%

f 764%

g 222%

h 1,285%

EXERCISE 7.3

a $\dfrac{7}{25}$

b $\dfrac{37}{100}$

c $\dfrac{5}{8}$

d $1\,{}^{7}\!/_{20}$

e 11

EXERCISE 7.4

a 0.085

b 0.4525

c 0.675

d 1.47

e 12.5

EXERCISE 7.5

a €9.38

b €1.13

c €1.93

d €23.80

e €20.37

f €57.99

EXERCISE 7.6

a €11.54

b €1.39

c €2.37

d €29.27

e €25.06

f €71.33

EXERCISE 7.7

	23%		13.5%		8%	
	VAT €	Goods €	VAT €	Goods €	VAT €	Goods €
a	3.74	16.26	2.38	17.62	1.48	18.52
b	6.54	28.46	4.16	30.84	2.59	32.41
c	23.37	101.63	14.87	110.13	9.26	115.74

EXERCISE 8.2

a   46m

b   96m

c   35m

EXERCISE 8.3

a

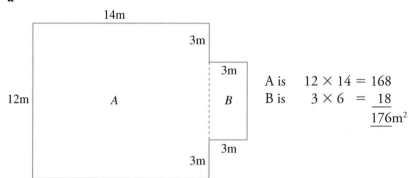

A is   12 × 14 = 168
B is   3 × 6 = 18
                    176m²

b

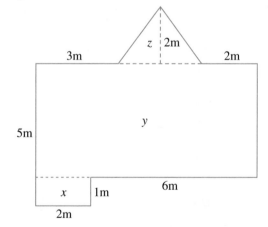

x is 2 × 1   =   2m²
y is 5 × (6 + 2)
        5 × 8   = 40m²
z is .5 × 3 × 2   =   3m²
                        45m²

c

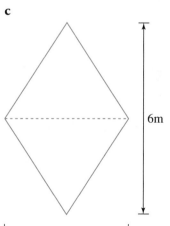

Divide shape into 2 equal triangles
Each is .5 base × height = .5 × 4 × 3 = 6m
                    2 × 6 = 12m²

d

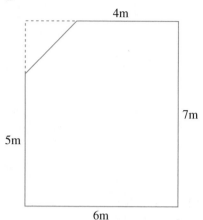

The entire rectangle is $6 \times 7 = 42m^2$
Less the triangle, which is
2m base and 2m ht
So, $.5 \times 2 \times 2 =$ $\underline{2m^2}$
                              $\underline{40m^2}$

e

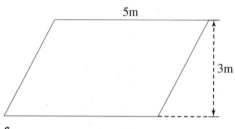

Area is $5 \times 3 = 15m^2$

f

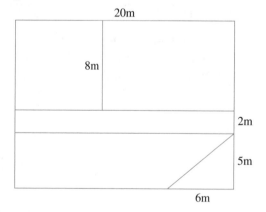

(i)   Whole park $20 \times (8 + 2 + 5)$
                      $= 20 \times 15 = 300m^2$
(ii) Play area is 8×8 $= 64$
(iii) Path is 2 m $\times$ 20 $= 40$
(iv) Flowerbed is $.5 \times 6 \times 5$ $= \underline{15}$
         Total so far $\underline{119m^2}$
(v)   Grass is therefore $300 - 119 = 181m^2$

EXERCISE 8.4

a 37.68m
b 28.26m
c 12.56m
d 21.98m
e 94.2cm
f 72.2mm

EXERCISE 8.5

a 113.04m²
b 63.59m²
c 12.56m²
d 38.47m²
e 706.5cm²
f 415.27mm²

EXERCISE 8.6

a 216cm^3
b 27m^3
c 24m^3
d 60m^3

EXERCISE 8.7

a 1,200cm^3
b 90m^3
c 93.75m^3
d 2.25m^3
e 8,177cm^3
f 0.014m^3 or 14,000cm^3

EXERCISE 8.8

a 37.68m^3
b 5.3m^3
c 2.45m^3

d 0.025m^3
e 226.08m^3
f 25.12m^3

EXERCISE 8.9

a 340.69cm^2
b 7.85m^2

EXERCISE 8.10

a 7,065cm^3
b 847.8cm^3
c 5.89m^3
d 379.42m^3
e 0.0157m^3
f (c) 5,890 litres
  (d) 379,420 litres
  (e) 15.7 litres

EXERCISE 9.1

a	Alan	38.5 effective hours @ 12.50	€481.25
b	Brian	46.25 effective hours @ 14.00	€647.50
c	Carol	56 effective hours @ 15.80	€884.80
d	Deirdre	46 effective hours @ 17.50	€805.00

EXERCISE 9.2

a	Amy	(120 × 4) + (25 × 6)	€630.00
b	Brendan	(15 × 28.50) + (6 × 40)	€667.50
c	Carlos	(25 × 20) + (3 × 27.50)	€582.50
d	Donna	(52 × 7.50) + (12 × 10)	€510.00

EXERCISE 9.3

a	Eric	250 + (26,300 @ 2.5%)	€907.50
b	Frances	400 + (32,300 @ 15%)	€5,245.00
c	Geraldine	€2,675 @ 25%	€668.75
d	Harriet	€56,500 @ 3.5%	€1,977.50

EXERCISE 9.4

Tax Deduction Card

Employee Name: Peter O'Connor			PPS Number: 123456T				Tax Credit €3,300		Total Cut-off €32,000						
	G	H	I	J	K	L	M	N	O	P	Q	C	D	E	
Wk No	Gross Pay Less Superannuation	Cumulative Gross Pay to Date	Cumulative Standard Rate Cut-off Point	Cumulative Tax Due at Standard Rate	Cumulative Tax Due at Higher Rate	Cumulative Gross Tax	Cumulative Tax Credit	Cumulative Tax (cannot be less than 0)	Tax Deducted This Period	Tax Refunded This Period	Total USC	PRSI (ee)	PRSI Total	For Employers Use	PRSI Class
1	550.00	550.00	615.38	110.00	nil	110.00	63.46	46.54	46.54		17.15	22.00	81.13	59.13	A1
2	735.00	1,285.00	1,230.76	246.15	22.24	268.39	126.92	141.47	94.93		38.56	29.40	108.41	79.01	A1
3	330.00	1,615.00	1,846.14	323.00	nil	323.00	190.38	132.62		8.85	10.21	13.20	48.68	35.48	AL
4	878.00	2,493.00	2,461.52	492.30	12.91	505.21	253.85	251.36	118.75		40.11	35.12	129.51	94.39	A1
5			3,076.90				317.31								
6			3,692.28				380.77								
7			4,307.66				444.23								
8			4,923.04				507.69								
9			5,538.42				571.15								
10			6,153.80				634.62								
11			6,769.18				698.08								
12			7,384.56				761.54								
13			7,999.94				825.00								
14			8,615.32				888.46								
15			9,230.70				951.92								
16			9,846.08				1,015.38								
17			10,461.46				1,078.85								
18			11,076.84				1,142.31								
19			11,692.22				1,205.77								
20			12,307.60				1,269.23								
21			12,922.98				1,332.69								
22			13,538.36				1,396.15								
23			14,153.74				1,459.62								
24			14,769.12				1,523.08								
25			15,384.50				1,586.54								
26			15,999.88				1,650.00								

Note: This sample shows just 26 weeks (half a year).

EXERCISE 10.1

	23%	13.50%	8%
	€	€	€
a	0.56	0.36	0.22
b	1.31	0.83	0.52
c	2.24	1.43	0.89
d	4.30	2.74	1.70
e	3.27	2.08	1.30
f	5.41	3.44	2.14
g	14.71	9.35	5.83
h	12.25	7.79	4.85
i	23.71	15.08	9.39
j	47.95	30.50	19.00
k	74.61	47.46	29.56
l	230.85	146.94	91.45

EXERCISE 11.1

a €975.00
b €1,080.00
c €546.25
d €350.00
e €9,246.78

EXERCISE 11.2

Date	Details	Lodged	Withdrawn	Balance
Day 1	Initial lodgement	1,000		1,000
Year 1	Interest for year	100		1,100
Year 2	Interest for year	100		1,200
Year 3	Interest for year	100		1,300

EXERCISE 11.3

a €2,083.50, €6,083.50
b €2,271.08, €8,571.08
c €3,313.35, €7,063.35
d €4317.97, €22,192.97
e €10,000

EXERCISE 11.4

a €1,805.40
b €30.60
c €3.05
d €838.38
e €801.11

EXERCISE 11.5

a

20% Straight line €	Car (5 years)	20% Reducing balance €
12,000	Cost	12,000
2,400	Dep'n year 1	2,400
9,600	Net book value year 1	9,600
2,400	Dep'n year 2	1,920
7,200	Net book value year 2	7,680
2,400	Dep'n year 3	1,536
4,800	Net book value year 3	6,144
2,400	Dep'n year 4	1,229
2,400	Net book value year 4	4,915
2,400	Dep'n year 5	983
Nil	Net book value year 5	€3,932

Cars are always depreciated using the reducing balance method. This applies to the motor trade and to accounting practice.

b

10% Straight line €	Mahogany table (10 years)	10% Reducing balance €
7,000	Cost	7,000
600	Dep'n year 1	700
6,400	Net book value year 1	6,300
600	Dep'n year 2	630
5,800	Net book value year 2	5,670
600	Dep'n year 3	567
5,200	Net book value year 3	5,103

Reducing balance is probably best here, as the table is worth less each year.

(Depreciated on €6,000 only)

c

25% Straight line €	Computer (4 years)	25% Reducing balance €
8,500	Cost	8,500
2,000	Dep'n year 1	2,125
6,500	Net book value year 1	6,375
2,000	Dep'n year 2	1,594
4,500	Net book value year 2	4,781
2,000	Dep'n year 3	1,195
2,500	Net book value year 3	3,586
2,000	Dep'n year 4	896
500	Net book value year 4	2,690

This example shows that the reducing balance method requires much higher percentage rates to get close to low residual values, even after 4 years at 25%. In this case, straight line is definitely the better option.

d

25% Straight line €	Software (4 years)	25% Reducing balance €
5,800	Cost	5,800
1,450	Dep'n year 1	1,450
4,350	Net book value year 1	4,350
1,450	Dep'n year 2	1,088
2,900	Net book value year 2	3,263
1,450	Dep'n year 3	816
1,450	Net book value year 3	2,447
1,450	Dep'n year 4	612
0	Net book value year 4	1,835

As above. Again, straight line is best.

e

20% Straight line €	Sandpit (5 years)	20% Reducing balance €
95,000	Cost	120,000
19,000	Dep'n year 1	24,000
76,000	Net book value year 1	96,000
19,000	Dep'n year 2	19,200
57,000	Net book value year 2	76,800
19,000	Dep'n year 3	15,360
38,000	Net book value year 3	61,440
19,000	Dep'n year 4	12,288
19,000	Net book value year 4	49,152
19,000	Dep'n year 5	9,830
nil	Net book value year 5	39,322

€25,000 Residual value remains

The sandpit will run out of sand, given normal production, in the 5 years. Straight line is better. Some businesses would allocate the depreciation based on tons produced in each year rather than on either of our systems.

Rate still too low.

EXERCISE 12.1

a

Income Budget for Alan and Breda Connolly for April to June		April €	May €	June €	Total €
INCOME:					
Michael	Veg sales	1,200	1,200	3,000	5,400
	Musician	300	300	300	900
Mary	Salary	3,500	3,500	3,500	10,500
	Bonus		2,000		2,000
TOTAL INCOME		5,000	7,000	6,800	18,800

b

Income Budget for Donal and Elisa Flanagan for July to September		July €	August €	September €	Total €
INCOME:					
Donal	Salary	2,200	1,980	1,980	6,160
Elisa	Salary	1,750	1,750	1,750	5,250
Child Benefit		240	240	240	720
TOTAL INCOME		4,190	3,970	3,970	12,130

Notice Donal's pay cut is calculated and only the expected amount shown.

c

Income Budget for Geraldine and Harry Ingles Quarter Ended 31 December	October €	November €	December €	Total €
INCOME:				
Regular take-home	4,000	4,000	4,000	12,000
Football club		250	300	550
Holiday fund			6,000	6,000
TOTAL INCOME	4,000	4,250	10,300	18,550

EXERCISE 12.2

Budget for John and Kay Lahart January to April					
	January €	February €	March €	April €	Total €
INCOME:					
John	2,500	2,500	2,500	2,500	10,000
Kay	3,000	3,000	3,000	3,000	12,000
TOTAL INCOME	5,500	5,500	5,500	5,500	22,000
EXPENSES:					
Fixed:					
Rent	1,250	1,250	1,250	1,250	5,000
Car loan	750	750	750	750	3,000
Health insurance			2,500		2,500
Variable:					
Energy bills		350		350	700
Groceries	1,000	1,000	1,000	1,000	4,000
Discretionary:					
Savings credit union	1,000	1,000	1,000	1,000	4,000
Holiday		2,500			2,500
TOTAL INCOME	4,000	6,850	6,500	4,350	21,700
SURPLUS FOR THE WEEK	1,500	(1,350)	(1,000)	1,150	300
Opening balance	500	2,000	650	(350)	500
Closing balance	2,000	650	(350)	800	800

Note: There's a bank overdraft expected in March. They might want to avoid that by curtailing their spending in Paris a little!

EXERCISE 12.3

a

Budget for Quentin and Roxanne Sullivan January to April					
	January €	February €	March €	April €	Total €
INCOME:					
Quentin	3,200	3,360	3,360	3,360	13,280
Roxanne	6,000	6,000	6,000	6,000	24,000
Child Benefit	240	240	240	240	960
TOTAL INCOME	9,440	9,600	9,600	9,600	38,240
EXPENSES:					
Fixed:					
Mortgage	2,000	2,000	2,000	2,000	8,000
Car loan	1,200	1,200	1,200	1,200	4,800
Health insurance			3,000		3,000
Pension plan	2,000	2,000	2,000	2,000	8,000
Variable:					
Heating & telephone	550		600		1,150
Groceries	1,250	1,250	1,250	1,250	5,000
Petrol	600	600	600	600	2,400
Childminding	800	800	800	800	3,200
Clothes (1)	700	700	700	700	2,800
Discretionary:					
Cruise				4,000	4,000
Birthday party	1,000				1,000
TOTAL INCOME	10,100	8,550	12,150	12,550	43,350
Net cash flow (2)	(660)	1,050	(2,550)	(2,950)	(5,110)
Opening balance	10,000	9,340	10,390	7,840	10,000
Closing balance	9,340	10,390	7,840	4,890	4,890

Notes:
(1) Clothes could be considered as discretionary by some and essential by others. That's a lifestyle choice but makes no difference to the budget. They still spend the money!
(2) If they don't make some changes soon, they will run out of cash. The budget shows overspending in three of the four months.

b (i)

Budget for Una and Val Walker May to July				
	May €	June €	July €	Total €
INCOME:				
Una	1,400	1,456	1,456	4,312
Val	1,800	1,872	1,872	5,544
Bonus	500			500
TOTAL INCOME	3,700	3,328	3,328	10,356
EXPENSES:				
Fixed:				
Rent	1,300	1,300	1,300	3,900
Insurance			300	300
Variable:				
Electricity	200		150	350
Groceries	600	600	600	1,800
Travelling	180	180	180	540
Lunches	200	200	200	600
Mobile phones	160	160	160	480
Discretionary:				
Credit union	500	500	500	1,500
Holiday in Italy			1,400	1,400
Pocket money	400	400	400	1,200
TOTAL INCOME	3,540	3,340	5,190	12,070
Net cash flow (2)	160	(12)	(1,862)	(1,714)
Opening balance	600	760	748	600
Closing balance	760	748	(1,114)	(1,114)

(ii) They will not have enough as things stand.

(iii) They could use some of their credit union savings. They could look for some overtime or part-time work. They could bring a packed lunch to work and ease up on pocket-money spending.

EXERCISE 12.4

Budget for Pye's Building Supplies for January to March				
	January €	February €	March €	Total €
Sales (memo only)	10,000	12,000	15,000	37,500
Income				
Debtors (last month's sales)	–	10,000	12,000	22,000
VAT refund		350		350
	–	10,350	12,000	22,350
Expenses				
Creditors (2 months owed) (1)	–	–	5,000	5,000
Niall & Orla	1,600	1,600	1,600	4,800
PAYE		1,000		1,000
Property tax	200			200
Waste charges			150	150
Commission 10% sales	1,000	1,200	1,500	3,700
Delivery etc. 5%	500	600	750	1,850
Phone	100	100	100	300
Electricity and gas	200		350	550
Other business expenses	2,000	2,000	2,000	6,000
Total expenses	5,600	6,500	11,450	23,550
Net cash flow	(5,600)	3,850	550	(1,200)
Opening balance	5,000	(600)	3,250	5,000
Closing balance	€(600)	€3,250	€3,800	€3,800

EXERCISE 13.1

	Mark-up	Selling price
a	€0.60	€2.10
b	€0.75	€4.50
c	€7.50	€20.00
d	€57.60	€129.60
e	€1,500.00	€2,700.00

EXERCISE 13.2

	Mark-up	% on cost
a	€0.30	25.0%
b	€1.06	40.0%
c	€28.80	80.0%
d	€39.60	110.0%
e	€65.00	39.4%

EXERCISE 13.3

a	€3.60
b	€1.45
c	€44.00
d	€421.48
e	€2,350.00

EXERCISE 13.4

	Gross profit	% of sales
a	€0.50	25.0%
b	€3.75	50.0%
c	€6.25	33.3%
d	€88.00	55.0%
e	€1,300.00	52.0%

EXERCISE 13.5

	Cost price	Gross profit %
a	€0.75	50%
b	€1.30	65%
c	€42.10	35%
d	€57.45	24%
e	€102.47	72%

EXERCISE 13.6

	Cost price	Selling price
a	€8.00	€16.00
b	€82.50	€110.00
c	€77.00	€110.00
d	€10.89	€38.89
e	€25.62	€124.99

EXERCISE 13.7

Rate per euro:	$1.31	£0.81	CHF 1.21
Euros	Dollars	Sterling	Swiss Francs
a €6.60	$8.65	£5.35	CHF 6.47
b €365.00	$478.15	£387.30	CHF 468.63
c €1,325.50	$1,736.41	£1,406.49	CHF 1,701.85
d €26,856.65	$35,182.21	£28,497.59	CHF 34,482.09

EXERCISE 13.8

a	€6.89
b	€22.40
c	€112.28
d	€10,744.82
e	€8.52
f	€50.30
g	€364.86
h	€15,542.17
i	€5.23
j	€29.40
k	€442.18
l	€1,680.24

EXERCISE 13.9

a (i) €522.36
(ii) €97.68
(iii) €131.80
(iv) €292.89
(v) €357.18
(vi) €8.34 loss
b (i) €2,032.53
(ii) €630.80
(iii) 31% on sales
(iv) €1,401.72
(v) €1,149.43

EXERCISE 14.1

	(a)	(b)	(c)	(d)
Mode occurs most often	8	17	5,8	none
Median is middle value	6	15	13	17
Mean: arithmetic average	6.7	15.6	24	25.3

EXERCISE 14.2

a Mode 18 /////
  19 /
  20 ///
  21 /
  Mean 19

b Mode $\left\{ \begin{array}{l} \end{array} \right.$ 7 ///// 35
  8 ///// 40 8.1875
  9 //// 36
  10 // 20
  Mean 8.2

c A /////// Mode
  B /
  C //////
  D //////
  E ////
  n/a Mean
  (A, B, C, etc. are not values!)

d Mean: 44.4 years

   Mode: 52 years

e

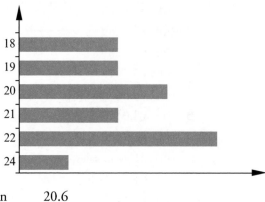

Mean   20.6

Mode   22

EXERCISE 14.3

a Early retirement group

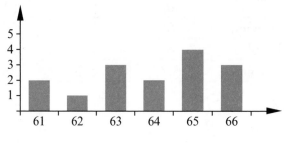

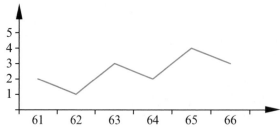

b   Golf scores

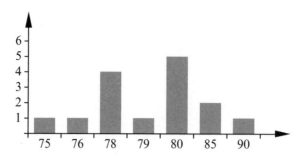

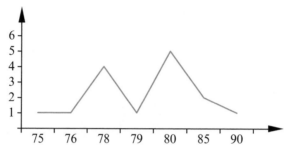

EXERCISE 15.1

a   (i) $\log_3 9 = 2$

(ii) $\log_2 8 = 3$

(iii) $\log_3 243$

b   (i) $81 = 3^4$

(ii) $32 = 2^5$

(iii) $27 = 3^3$

c   (i) $\log_3 x = 4, x = 3^4, x = 81$

(ii) $\log_3 9 = x, 9 = 3^x, x = 2$

(iii) $\log_x 25 = 2, 25 = x^2, x = 5$

d   (i) $\dfrac{\log_x m}{\log_x k}$

(ii) $\dfrac{\log_x 7}{\log_x 2}$

e   (i) $\log_a x + \log_a y$

(ii) $\log_a 2 - \log_a 3$

(iii) $2 \log_a 5$

f   (i) $\log (xy)^2$

(ii) $\log \left(\dfrac{x^2}{y^3} \right)$